R M SMITH

Union Hypocrisy

Organized Labors Double Standard in Business and Politics

ISBN: 1-4782-7516-2
ISBN-13: 9781478275169

DEDICATION

This is dedicated to and in memory of Van Fleming, the only person I would rob a bank with

To my husband Jeff, my rock my best friend.

If the UNIONs are NOBLE in their Campaign Cause and unionization really is the best choice, what possibly could I or anyone else do to override their proclaimed status?
—Anonymous

CONTENTS

PROLOGUE

April 2008

The corporation distributed the following documents to its employees in their sales division offices across the United States. These documents were given to employees regardless of their seniority or sales experience. Without the benefit of negotiations or a contractual bargaining agreement, they were being informed for the first time that they could be terminated at will. The salespeople were now to be considered temporary field employees.

The forms that came out closely resembled the following:

1. **Affirmation Page.** "By my signature below, I acknowledge that I have read the Corporation's Code of Conduct ("Code"), and that I understand my responsibilities written within the Code. I understand that the Code has been issued for informational purposes only and that it is not intended to create, nor does it represent, a contract of employment for any definite period of time." Note: Failure to read and/or sign this Affirmation will in no way relieve you of your responsibilities under the Code.

2. **Candidate Release Authorization.** This authorization gives the corporation written permission to obtain virtually all the salesperson's personal records, including, but not limited to, Workers Compensation Claims, statements about personal character, mode of living, court records, education, consumer credit history, driving record, past employment references, past employment reasons for termination, and much more.

3. **Temporary Field Employee Handbook Acknowledgment Form.** "I acknowledge that I have received, read, and understand the policies outlined in the Corporation's Temporary Field Employee Handbook, which is intended as a guide to policies and procedures. I understand that the Corporation has the right to change the Hand-

book without notice. It is understood that future changes in the policies and procedures will supersede or eliminate those found in the book, and that employees will be notified of such changes through normal communication channels. The Handbook was prepared to acquaint all temporary employees of the Corporation with its core employment policies and ethical standards of conduct.

"I also understand and agree that the information contained in these materials does not constitute an employment contract between the Corporation and me, and that either the Corporation or I may terminate our employment relationship at any time, with or without cause. I understand that no manager or representative of the Corporation, other than the CEO, the CFO, or their designees, has any authority to enter into any agreement for employment for any specified period of time, or to make any agreement contrary to the foregoing."

4. **A Letter from the Director of the Human Resources Department of the Corporation.** In the letter the HR director instructs the salespeople that the corporation has developed a new employment handbook setting out the employment policies and procedures that cover the corporation's salespeople. The employees are also informed that, in the future, they will be referred to as "Temporary Field Employees." Some instructions similar to the following are included in the letter:

• Employees are instructed that they will be required to "remain in compliance with its requirements."

• Employees will be required to divulge personal information, including the Social Security numbers of spouses and children.

All of this information, the letter reassures the reader, is for informational purposes only. (What else would it be for?)

5. **Medical Information Form.** This form requires the employee to provide the corporation with the name, address, Social Security number, gender, and marital status of their spouse and children. The following note is at the bottom of the page: "This information is requested for informational purposes only and will not be used to make decisions with respect to your temporary employment status.

6. **Memorandum.**
TO: Sales Campaign Coordinators
FROM: Operations Manager
DATE: September 17, 2008
RE: Employment Paper Work

This memorandum instructs the field employees to return all the required forms as a "part of the conditions of employment." The operations manager also acknowledges that many have not yet returned the forms, despite the department making follow-up calls and mailing letters to them in attempts to get them to sign.

7. **Release Form for Consumer Reports Temporary Field Employees.** This form gives the corporation permission to search additional sources for personal information about their employees in the sale department.

This corporation provided its employees with a stark example of corporate invasion of privacy. The vast majority of the employees in the sales department did not sign the forms. Instead, they discussed and rallied toward organizing into a recognized bargaining unit. A union.

As the employees talked among themselves and other employees, they found that they were not the only department affected by this new handbook it also applied to staff working in the political relations department. The corporation had brought in outside consultants and concocted these new employee standards, which made unilateral changes to the terms of employment for just about all corporate staffers. Corporate counsel and his wrecking crew would make more changes without bothering to negotiate them with employees. Some of the employees saw the warning signs of bad things to come when the corporate counsel fired the head of HR and replaced her with someone coming from outside the corporation—not in-house, as had been the tradition for over a hundred years. Maybe he could not find a qualified in-house applicant to fill the position. Some felt that their closely knit "family" was being corporatized. However, maybe they just never realized that had been a corporation for many years now.

Out of all the staff affected, it was the brash and bold members of the sales department who really created a scene—because most of the salespeople were passionate about their jobs, which is what made them good. Originally the department had two types of salespeople: those who were considered permanent full-time employees and those who were hired to work on a particular project—hence the term project salesperson. The project salespeople were hired for six months, which could be extended at six-month intervals. Over time, that became three-month terms with three-month extensions.

With the new handbook, it was down to thirty days, with the option of a thirty-day extension.

This corporation was quite wily when it came to reducing their exposure to employing permanent employees, thus limiting their exposure to unionization and allowing them reprieve from many of those annoying National Labor Relations Board (NLRB) rules. To further limit the potential for unionizing, project sales people were actually hired by subsidiaries and then "lent" to the Corporation. The Corporation would then reimburse the subsidiary for the cost of their wages. However, the health and welfare benefits would be covered by the subsidiary.

Now, with the mailing of handbooks to all project sale people, they will be classified as "temporary field employees" who are AT-WILL, giving the Corporation a means to terminate those employees without cause.

The staff sales people are official sales personnel of the Corporation because they receive their payroll check directly from the Corporation and fall under Medical & Pension Plans that the Corporation has in at its corporate headquarters.

Project sales people receive all work assignments from the Corporation. They are accountable to the Corporation and the Corporation pays for all expenses while the project salespeople are on the ground working. Expense reports get turned in to the Corporation. Monthly activity reports are turned in to the Corporation. A daily debrief sheet and weekly reports went to the corporation. The corporation provided the cell phones.

All salespeople, whether project or staff, performed the same work out in the field on any given day, in any targeted industry, anywhere in the USA, in both public and private sectors.

It seemed that the corporation had a complete grasp of the legal definition of subcontracting. Since the employees came from a multitude of subsidiaries from around the country, the corporation could, of course, claim that they did not employ them; after all, they never cut a payroll check to any of the project salespeople. These people all worked for separate, subordinate bodies.

Out of anger and rage against this abuse of their employment, salespeople could be heard voicing sentiments such as the "employee handbook"—as they called it—"is a piece of s**t!"

Ever since I started working for this b.s. corporation, I realized I had walked into a monument to corporate greed! I was tired of the empty promises, and sick of all the smoke being blown up my ass! My dream job was nothing but a horrible nightmare: no money, no respect, and no appreciation. To top it off, the people in charge had never worked in this industry! Are you kidding me? I was just a little upset with these conditions, as you can tell. We needed a contract! I refused to be considered an "at-will employee." I had never dreamed this would happen. I was ready to stand with my coworkers to form a union! Join me and others that know we need this. Stand up and be heard!

The corporation was another Wal-Mart.

"Temporary field employees" were "at-will" employees. Approximately 71 percent of the salespeople refused to sign their rights away. Therefore, the corporation began calling the project salespeople in attempts to coerce them into signing their rights away. That did not work. So then they asked the site lead salespeople to ask the people working on their team to sign the paperwork. When that did not work, sales campaign coordinators, who are management, were asked to get them to sign the paperwork. One-on-one meetings took place, and management made it clear: sign the paperwork or face termination.

On November 6, 2008, the corporation started firing.

Corporate greed and abuse was alive and well, finding loopholes in labor law. They were abusing their employees and giving them no voice at all in the terms of employment. Anti-union corporate America.

Which corporation "stuck it" to their employees? Which corporation insisted on at-will employment for their employees? Surely, this is an example of why employees need union representation. A union would insist on just cause; a union would force the corporation to respect its workers and give them job security. Was it Federal Express or maybe Wal-Mart? No. A corporation more anti-union than that perhaps?

Go back and replace the words *corporation* with International Brotherhood of Teamsters, *subsidiary* with union local, and *salesperson* with organizer.

What is good for corporate America is obviously not good for the international unions. And there are other unions just as guilty, such as the Service Employees International Union (SEIU).

In 2008, the Teamsters had been able to stamp down this dangerous union talk among its employees, but as of 2012, it was back again. On February 9, 2012, thirty-nine staff organizers filed a petition with the NLRB in Chicago, 8-RC-73341, for recognition under Teamsters Local 964. On March 19, 2012, the Federation for Agents and International Representatives (FAIR) filed a petition to also represent the same organizers.

In many ways, the unions have become hypocrites about their own mantra, and we will explore many cases in this book. Trade unionism (unions consisting of those who work in a trade or craft such as pipefitters or masons) has given way to political ideologue, and unions are just as guilty, if not more so, of making a buck on the backs of the working class. After all, corporate America has never hidden its agenda of being in it for the money, whereas unions promote the cause while marching to a different tune behind closed doors. There is no better example of how an organization can remain union-free than the unions themselves. The ultimate hypocrisy.

Book One
When Union Employees Organize

Chapter 1
Organized Labor Union Busting Teamsters

"We will be fighting for the rights of every American worker, private or public, to bargain collectively for better wages, benefits and working conditions."
—James Hoffa Jr., general president of the International Brotherhood of Teamsters, in the March 24, 2011, *Huffington Post*

Despite Jimmy Hoffa's quote, actually, the Teamsters union fights for every worker except the ones who work for the mighty International Brotherhood of Teamsters (IBT). Are the organizers second-class citizens? They don't count, I guess. Maybe they are second-class citizens within the grand marble halls of the IBT, known by its members as the "Marble Palace." People employed by the Teamsters don't have a right to bargain collectively for better wages, benefits, and working conditions, do they, Mr. Hoffa?

Organizers Attempt to Organize
In the situation described in the prologue, here's what happened: In January 2012, the Teamsters employees filed another petition to organize as a bargaining unit. (All told, there have been four attempts by the Teamsters organizers to organize themselves.) The bargaining unit consisted of the organizers themselves. The petition was filed in Chicago, but the international union declined to recognize the bargaining unit.

General President Hoffa's response was that he would recognize the organizers if they were represented by any union other than the Teamsters. As had happened in the past, the Teamsters engaged in evasive tactics to avoid recognizing their staff organizers as a union and commencing negotiations accordingly.

Another petition to organize was also filed by the Federation of Agents and International Representatives (FAIR). Just by having another union file a petition, the employees had split their vote three ways. If an election went forward, there would be three choices on the ballet: Teamsters Local 964, FAIR, and no union. This would greatly reduce the chance of any union winning representational rights for the bargaining unit, as the pro-union group would split itself between the two unions offered. Some believe that it was even those opposed to unionizing who signed the cards to bring in FAIR, thereby weakening the pro-union movement. It is believed this strategy was encouraged by the management of the International Brotherhood of Teamsters.

MAR-20-2012 07:45 NLRB WRO 202 208 3013 P.03

INTERNET FORM NLRB-502 (2-08)	UNITED STATES GOVERNMENT NATIONAL LABOR RELATIONS BOARD PETITION	DO NOT WRITE IN THIS SPACE
		Case No. 05-RC-076931 Date Filed 03/20/12

INSTRUCTIONS: Submit an original of this Petition to the NLRB Regional Office in the Region in which the employer concerned is located.

The Petitioner alleges that the following circumstances exist and requests that the NLRB proceed under its proper authority pursuant to Section 9 of the NLRA.

1. PURPOSE OF THIS PETITION (If box RC, RM, or RD is checked and a charge under Section 8(b)(7) of the Act has been filed involving the Employer named herein, the statement following the description of the type of petition shall not be deemed made.) (Check One)

☑ RC-CERTIFICATION OF REPRESENTATIVE - A substantial number of employees wish to be represented for purposes of collective bargaining by Petitioner and Petitioner desires to be certified as representative of the employees.

☐ RM-REPRESENTATION (EMPLOYER PETITION) - One or more individuals or labor organizations have presented a claim to Petitioner to be recognized as the representative of employees of Petitioner.

☐ RD-DECERTIFICATION (REMOVAL OF REPRESENTATIVE) - A substantial number of employees assert that the certified or currently recognized bargaining representative is no longer their representative.

☐ UD-WITHDRAWAL OF UNION SHOP AUTHORITY (REMOVAL OF OBLIGATION TO PAY DUES) - Thirty percent (30%) or more of employees in a bargaining unit covered by an agreement between their employer and a labor organization desire that such authority be rescinded.

☐ UC-UNIT CLARIFICATION-A labor organization is currently recognized by Employer, but Petitioner seeks clarification of placement of certain employees: (Check one) ☐ In unit not previously certified. ☐ In unit previously certified in Case No. _____

☐ AC-AMENDMENT OF CERTIFICATION- Petitioner seeks amendment of certification issued in Case No. _____ Attach statement describing the specific amendment sought.

2. Name of Employer: International Brotherhood of Teamsters	Employer Representative to contact: James Hoffa	Tel. No. 202-624-6800
		Fax No.

3. Address(es) of Establishment(s) involved (Street and number, city, State, ZIP code): 25 Louisiana Ave. N.W. Washington D.C. 20001-2198

4a. Type of Establishment (Factory, mine, wholesaler, etc.): Labor Union	4b. Identify principal product or service: Organizing	Cell No.	e-Mail

5. Unit involved (In UC petition, describe present bargaining unit and attach description of proposed clarification.)

Included: All full-time and part-time International Organizers of the International Brotherhood of Teamsters.

Excluded: All other office clerical, professional, and supervisory employees as defined by the act.

6a. Number of Employees in Unit: 40
Present:
Proposed (By UC/AC):

6b. Is this petition supported by 30% or more of the employees in the unit? ☑ Yes ☐ No
*Not applicable in RM, UC, and AC.

(If you have checked box RC in 1 above, check and complete EITHER item 7a or 7b, whichever is applicable)

7a. ☐ Request for recognition as Bargaining Representative was made on (Date) _____ and Employer declined recognition on or about (Date) _____ (If no reply received, so state).

7b. ☐ Petitioner is currently recognized as Bargaining Representative and desires certification under the Act.

8. Name of Recognized or Certified Bargaining Agent (If none, so state.): None
Address:
Affiliation:
Tel. No.
Cell No.
Date of Recognition or Certification
Fax No.
e-Mail

9. Expiration Date of Current Contract, if any (Month, Day, Year):

10. If you have checked box UD in 1 above, show here the date of execution of agreement granting union shop (Month, Day and Year):

11a. Is there now a strike or picketing at the Employer's establishment(s) involved? Yes ☐ No ☑
11b. If so, approximately how many employees are participating?

11c. The Employer has been picketed by or on behalf of (insert Name) _____ organization, of (insert Address) _____ a labor organization, of Since (Month, Day, Year) _____

12. Organizations or individuals other than Petitioner (and other than those named in items 8 and 11c), which have claimed recognition as representatives and other organizations and individuals known to have a representative interest in any employees in unit described in item 5 above. (If none, so state.)

Name	Address	Tel. No.	Fax No.
None		Cell No.	e-Mail

13. Full name of party filing petition (if labor organization, give full name, including local name and number): Federation Of Agents And International Representatives (F.A.I.R.)

14a. Address (street and number, city, state, and ZIP code): P.O. Box 760 Roseville, Ca 95661-0760
14b. Tel. No. EXT
14c. Fax No. 916-771-6990
14d. Cell No. 916-835-0928
14e. e-Mail bhmp@surewest.net

15. Full name of national or international labor organization of which Petitioner is an affiliate or constituent (to be filled in when petition is filed by a labor organization): None

I declare that I have read the above petition and that the statements are true to the best of my knowledge and belief. Date: 3-19-12

Name (Print): John W. Heise
Signature: [signature]
Title (if any): President
Address (street and number, city, state, and ZIP code): PO Box 760 Roseville, Ca. 95661-0760
Tel. No.
Fax No. 916-771-6990
Cell No. 916-835-0928
e-Mail bhmp@surewest.net

WILLFUL FALSE STATEMENTS ON THIS PETITION CAN BE PUNISHED BY FINE AND IMPRISONMENT (U.S. CODE, TITLE 18, SECTION 1001)

PRIVACY ACT STATEMENT

Solicitation of the information on this form is authorized by the National Labor Relations Act (NLRA), 29 U.S.C. § 151 et seq. The principal use of the information is to assist the National Labor Relations Board (NLRB) in processing unfair labor practice and related proceedings or litigation. The routine uses for the information are fully set forth in the Federal Register, 71 Fed. Reg. 74942-43 (Dec. 13, 2006). The NLRB will further explain these uses upon request. Disclosure of the information to the NLRB is voluntary; however, failure to supply the information will cause the NLRB to decline to invoke its processes.

MAR-20-2012 08:42   202 208 3013   97%   TOTAL P.03 / P.03

This promised to be quite a battle, and placed the Teamsters squarely in the position of the employer. The membership was divided; some sympathized with the organizers, and others sided with management—or should I say the International union? The IBT's stance on the matter was that if the organizers did not like how their job went, they were free to quit—just like everyone else in the organization. In addition, if any general president didn't like the way the organizers were working out, then he or she should be free to replace them as he or she saw fit and on behalf of the dues-paying members of the organization. Why should our union be handcuffed to these organizers if it has been determined that they can't organize?

Why indeed, as many employers (a.k.a. corporations) ask themselves and unions the same question when unions are either organizing or bargaining on behalf of the employees of that company. Companies also believe they should be able to replace employees when they are not working out. They also believe that their primary responsibility is to their stockholders. The Teamsters officials sounded just like the employers they rail against in their voice-for-the-workers speeches that they like to spew at every turn, or at least at any handy television camera. How ironic that they do not see the absurdity of what is happening. What is even more absurd is that, although they have no benefit of union protection, such that it is, these employees are still required to pay dues to keep their job. Teamsters gave a completely new meaning to pay-to-play.

The battle to organize has just begun, and already some organizers have asked for their union representation card back. A union representation card is a card that an employee would sign to show that the wish the union to bargain on their behalf with their employer. Did they get it back? One wonders because if workers change their mind and ask for their card back, they are pretty much out of luck. How do the Teamsters justify this to those they are organizing? Do they tell them it is because they wish to fire their workers whenever they want to, that they should not be stuck with an employee that is not working out? Does this sound hypocritical to anyone else but me? This could make every Teamsters campaign that much harder now. How are workers going to trust these organizers when they do not even have a Teamsters contract protecting their rights? Will Hoffa ask his loyal organizers to turn into union-busters if things look like they could go all the way to a union vote?

Rank-and-file members, for the most part, are backing their organizers. Some Teamsters members believed that their union's organizers were already represented with a contract. How can Hoffa sit in his marble palace and not acknowledge the very people on the front lines for the union? The very people who hold the responsibility for the union's growth in their hands? Hoffa's main campaign rhetoric when he was running for general president of the union his father built was to organize, organize, and organize. However, Hoffa has run the grand old institution like, well, like SEIU. SEIU has a reputation for being dictatorial and working their staff like dogs. Somewhere along the way, the Teamsters took a left turn and kept turning left.

It started in May 2006, when the Teamsters organizing department lineup looked something like this: Jeff Farmer, head of the organizing department, formerly with SEIU; Louie Rada, formerly or currently with SEIU; Celia Petty, formerly with AFL-CIO; Kim Keller, formerly with AFL-CIO Voice At Work; Rebecca Hanscom, formerly with SEIU; Carol Colbeth, formerly with AFSCME; Michael Filler, formerly with the National Treasury Employees Union (NTEU); Claudia Rozenberg, formerly with AFL-CIO Voice At Work; David Welker, formerly with Food and Allied Service Trades Department (FAST) of the AFL-CIO; Andy Banks, formerly with International Federation of Professional and Technical Engineers (IFPTE), AFL-CIO; Iain Gold, formerly with United Food and Commercial Workers (UFCW); Tim Beatty, formerly with AFL-CIO International Affairs; Kristin King, formerly with Marriott Corporation's human resources department; James Kimball, formerly with Old Dominion Electric Cooperative and the Virginia Department of Transportation; Chris Bartolomeo, formerly with the National Education Association (NEA); Matthew Mayers, formerly with the Association of Community Organizations for Reform Now (ACORN); Richard Lebo, formerly on the campaign staff for Lyndon LaRouche; Gregory Tarpinian, former member of the Communist Party USA (CPSU) and SEIU 1199 consultant; Jon Hartough; Peter O'Neill; Per

Bernstein; Galen Monroe; Shawn Ellis, formerly with AFL-CIO community services and former Teamster; John Slatery and Trisha Edwards, both formerly with UFCW; Manny Valenzuela, IBT; Dieter Waizenegger, AFL-CIO Office of Investment; Bret Caldwell, formerly with National Abortion and Reproductive Rights Action League (NARAL); and Ronald Carver, formerly with United Electrical, Radio, and Machine Workers of America (UE). The Teamsters had a tradition of hiring organizers from within, people who knew the culture and the trades the teamsters often represented so many saw this as a sign that Hoffa was trying to formatively change the Teamster Union.

The rank and file were left out in the cold as Hoffa sought to change the structure of the International. How can the Teamsters, with Hoffa at the helm, not be embarrassed by what is happening within its own ranks? Shouldn't the members' dues go towards strengthen the union and thereby strengthening the members' bargaining advantage? As it stands now, the dues have gone toward creating a corporate structure to rival any company on the Forbes list. Unfortunately, the members were the last to know.

Hoffa is turning the mission of organized labor into a joke, but his own organizers are not laughing.

In the past, IBT organizers originated from the locals. There was no organizing department because every local staff member was expected to organize. Organizing was recognized as the lifeblood of the union and considered the highest achievement among union members. Organizers were a part of every meeting, every strategy session. They were the best of the best and held in high esteem. Everyone respected those who had the skills in or were talented at the craft of organizing. For it was these master craftspeople, these wizards of the organizing trade, who formed new locals throughout the United States.

Then the International created an organizing department with general organizers. These members were also considered the cream of the crop. "Organize or die" was not just a chant; it was a heartfelt sentiment at the core of every union. Oh, but times changed and so did the hierarchy in the union.

It cannot be denied that organizers in the teamsters receive no respect and are often ridiculed. Something happened and a transition occurred where now the union business agent is perceived as the apex of achievement. The other change was that not all staffers were expected to be organizers. There is nothing that guarantees them any security in the position, there is no grievance procedure or a form of progressive discipline, which are basic employee manual articles that are even found at non-union companies.

The fact of the matter is that human resources policies at the union closely resemble the same as those at Wal-Mart, a company it abhors and launches negative public relations campaigns against. The union continues to enforce an "at-will" employment status with its organizers.

Teamsters management does not tolerate "at-will" status in their collective bargaining agreements, but it believes it is above having to conform to the same rule it insists companies follow.

In the latest organizing effort, not all organizers have signed a card, and some are actively campaigning against it. Does that make them scabs? This is what they accuse those employees of being who choose to vote against the union in the companies they attempt to organize. The union's numbers have dropped dramatically since the 1970s, when the International took over organizing. It was also when the union started targeting organizing efforts instead of preserving a presence in all areas. It is reported that locals dedicate less than 15 percent of their resources to organizing. Many have a limited organizing staff or even require an organizer to also act as a business agent.

Could it be that all hell is about break loose inside the International Brotherhood of Teamsters? Members are already asking, "Who are we—the SEIU?" I think Hoffa answered that question back in 2006 with the organizers who were brought on and giving Jeff Farmer the reins of the organizing department.

After all the "Stop the War on Workers," "Employee Free Choice Act," and Teamsters standing for worker rights/justice campaigns, Hoffa didn't even blink before denying recognition for his own organizers. Every day the union's mantra has been to "stand up for your rights and confront your boss." Lip service is the new trend at the Teamsters; rumors have been floating that the top-level people in the IBT's organizing department are now promoting the use of union-busting tactics toward organizers wanting union representation.

IBT organizers are just like the workers they are trying to organize. The lost timers (members who get a salary but no benefits) and the so-called "project organizers" have it worst. On the West Coast, Manny Valenzuela, the West Coast organizing director, allegedly lays off longtime organizers, with no recall rights, before they can be made full-time staffers. They are told it is due to budget constraints. However, Manny hires their replacements before the senior organizers are even out the door. This report comes from a man who was awarded the Joe Hill Award in 2005. (Joe Hill was a labor activist and a member of the "wobblies" at the turn of the twentieth century.) It appears that the union likes to tell others what they should do to take care of their employees' rights, but fails to take care of its own.

According to what members are saying, Manny Valenzuela has been personally calling organizers and trying to convince them that they do not need union protection. Using the same strategies that he and his staff have condemned as union busting, he is talking with and visiting organizers to discourage all talk of a union. Don't you wish you were a fly on that wall? Using union-busting tactics to stop an organizer from joining a union—that takes some cajones. How can you ask workers to sign a union representation card when you are telling your own employees not to sign one? Do the organizing department managers tell the organizers that even though they signed a card, they can still vote no in the union election? Alternatively, do they say, hey, we only have to meet with your union in good faith; we are under no obligation by law to ever agree to anything proposed by the union representing you? What can the Teamsters' internal buster say to an organizer? Do the organizers not recognize an anti-union campaign? How can you tell workers they need a union when you tell the union's employees they do not need one? Is there an implied threat that those organizers wanting a union will lose their jobs if a union is voted in? Do organizers feel a level of fear that their jobs are at risk if they sign a union authorization card? Oh, the questions I would love to ask, but will never get the chance to.

Perhaps many organizers are afraid they will lose their job if they support a union of their own. By the end of January 2012, a rank-and-file member who was an organizer out of Local 952 was fired and replaced. It is not clear whether he was let go for supporting a union—mostly because it is illegal to terminate employees for their union activities. Employees can state they were let go for this reason, but most employers, including the union, are savvy enough to make sure that the reason they put down in writing is something they can back up. No employee is perfect, and many times employers will overlook small lapses in judgment without any repercussions. However, when employers are looking for a reason to terminate workers' employment, they turn to what most who have been in a union refer to as "working to the rule." Quite simply it means that any violation, no matter how small, is written up. In the case of the Teamsters organizers, if they are at-will, or "project organizers," their employment is even more tenuous. They only have to be informed that their project is over—which is what happened to one organizer who supported unionizing the Teamsters. He soon found himself dismissed, the union saying his project was over, but the campaign he was on continued.

Former organizers who spoke up during this campaign have found themselves ostracized and on the receiving end of crude and unfounded allegations. A former female organizer stated on Teamster.net that she had not spoken up before, but found she could no longer hold it in, "since I resigned as an IBT organizer; claiming illness. I could no longer talk the talk and not walk the walk...I worked my ass off as my fellow organizers and was treated like a piece of ****! I was promoted, did well but left due to treatment and hypocrisy. Win, my friends, or unveil the absolute hypocrisy while trying."

Shortly after making that statement, she fielded a barrage of attacks on that chat board. One member responded by accusing her of sleeping with various employees from the union. In reviewing most of the attacks, if you are a female, 99 percent of them will be derogatory sexual remarks and demeaning comments implying you are a woman of loose morals who sleeps around. These types of attacks are only limited to women, so it appears to me that the Teamsters may have a bit of an issue with women—but hey, maybe they believe women like being referred to as sluts. The maneuver is obviously done by members who carry the International's water and is an attempt to discredit or embarrass women who speak out, so they'll shut up.

Another former female organizer, also stated her position on Teamster.net during this latest effort to organize: "You were all warned this was going to happen. The FIRINGS began in November 2008 with the FIRST campaign to organize the IBT Field Organizers, immediately following the first picture and quote that went to JAMES P. HOFFA.

"For any of you HUMAN BEINGS, and I don't care if you're a Rank and File Teamster or on your first WEEK as a MANNY MISFIT...HOFFA was approached on three occasions with a REQUEST to RECOGNIZE the unit and he said NO...NO...AND HELL NO!"

According to this former organizer, she was present when Hoffa was asked in 2008 to recognize the union, and she served on the 2008 organizing committee.

Some of the members complain, but none will take responsibility for what their union has become. Sounds remotely like our government. The Teamsters are too busy raiding other unions and fighting each other for political stature to realize the unjust actions of their own officials.

How amazing that the rank-and-file members either believe that employees of the union should be able to be replaced at will, or believe they should have the opportunity to be covered by contractual bargaining but refuse to stand up and fight for their own organizing staff.

In 2008, when the organizers stepped up to demand recognition as a bargaining unit, many ended up fighting a battle that lasted eighteen months. Those few who stood up were fighting for their representational rights. The organizers of 2012 were warned by those who attempted to be recognized as a bargaining unit in 2008. Had anyone paid attention back then, they would have seen the writing on the wall. Those organizers of 2008 predicted what would happen to the organizers of 2012 who attempted their own union-organizing effort. They showed that the International Brotherhood of Teamsters no longer believed in solidarity, no longer held sacred the ethics that its own constitution supposedly embraced. Just like the top management of any company dedicated to remaining union-free, the International Brotherhood of Teamsters has its "management" working the doors of its organizers, utilizing the union-busting tactics they loathe when used against them by a company. And like those companies, the International Brotherhood of Teamsters can be labeled anti-union.

It is hard to understand why some of the organizers are not standing with their coworkers. Along with the name calling, there have been a few chat board posts that touch on the real reasons for wanting a union, including having a grievance procedure, a voice on the job, and job security; changing the "at-will" to "just-cause" employment status; respect and dignity. Many organizers are asking the membership they represent, "Do you work under a CBA (contractual bargaining agreement) with representation? Are you willing to give that up? Would you work without a CBA?"

Most of the organizers agree that their stance has nothing to do with money or benefits. Many organizers believe it is an honor to organize for the union where they are employed. They believe in Norma Rae and the fight for employee rights in the face of ever-powerful corporate conglomerates. They believe they are making a difference. They are called pure trade unionists—and they do not survive long within the belly of the union beast. They are strangely naïve about the politics that must be played, as well as the deals with employers that must be cut. Their belief is so fierce and so pure, they truly believe that if they do their job well and inject their natural passion, they are safe from all other things and above the political fray that is engaged in, with enthusiastic viciousness, within the marble palace. The challenge that is present with the constant threat of the at-will status of employment is the catalyst for this drive. What it all boils down to is being Teamsters in the organizer job classification. In other words: living what you preach.

An organizer for the Teamsters goes through a background check, credit checks, and DMV checks. If they are hired, they receive a letter similar to this one:

> Dear Mr.——
> I am pleased to advise you that we have accepted your application for employment with the International Brotherhood of Teamsters as an International Organizer in our Organizing Department. As you were advised, the monthly starting salary will be _____(annualized at _____). This is a Class II, non-bargaining unit position, classified as professional. Enclosed with this employment offer letter are two (2) copies of your job description. Please review the document and sign your name on the applicable page. The second is for your reference files.

Can anyone at the International Brotherhood of Teamsters please explain why their own organizers do not deserve to have a grievance procedure or just cause covered by a contractual bargaining agreement?

As one member posted on Teamster.net in support of the organizers, "What was in the past is no longer today as in many things with our great union...If we want to hear the excuses he is giving for why someone should not have a CBA we might as well talk to management from Fed Ex. One sentence: are you a rank and file member that does not believe that EVERY WORKER should be represented by a Union and have a CBA; he believes that some workers should be AT WILL employees."

As this chapter is being written, those organizers being referred to as nonunion or ass-kissers are calling other organizers and encouraging them to vote no in the upcoming election. It is a matter of personal choice for an organizer to decide to sign or not sign a union representation card. However, when does an employee of the International Brotherhood of Teamsters cross the line and engage in union-busting tactics? If an employer engages in or hires someone to engage in the same activities, Hoffa decries this as union busting—as he did in the following letter to US Airways about its subsidiary hiring a union-avoidance firm. This letter was also posted on the Piedmont agents site that is sponsored by the Communication Workers of America.

INTERNATIONAL BROTHERHOOD of TEAMSTERS

JAMES P. HOFFA
General President

25 Louisiana Avenue, NW
Washington, DC 20001

C. THOMAS KEEGEL
General Secretary-Treasurer

202.624.6800
www.teamster.org

August 25, 2010

Mr. Doug Parker, Chairman
US Airways
111 West Rio Salado Parkway
Tempe, AZ 85281

Dear Mr. Parker:

It is with deep concern that I learned that Piedmont Airlines, the wholly owned subsidiary of USAir Group, has retained the services of renowned anti-union consultants, LRI. The purpose is of course to defeat the efforts of the Piedmont workers to form a union and allow them to bargain collectively for their wages and working conditions.

You may assert that this is simply a business decision, but we believe it is a very poor business decision. The long term damage to employee relations is incalculable and will be with you for years to come, regardless of the outcome of the pending representation election.

All employees of USAir Group work very hard every day to make this airline a success. Most of those employees have long ago chosen union representation and developed a productive working relationship with those who manage the various airlines within the Group. The retention of LRI and the intense anti-union campaign they are waging offers an unpleasant insight into the reality of how the executives of USAir Group view their represented employees.

I urge you to insist that Piedmont management save the money they are paying LRI and invest it instead in the airline and its valuable employees. I believe that a failure to do so will result in long term ramifications including the rejection of future requests for cooperation and shared sacrifice from those who have been insulted and attacked in the course of the LRI campaign.

Please feel free to contact me if you wish to discuss these concerns further.

Sincerely,

James P. Hoffa
General President

JPH:nd
cc: David Bourne, Teamsters Airline Division

Does the union have a split personality? Do the Teamsters want or not want every worker to have a contract? In the above letter, Hoffa states that they believe this type of action by the employer will result in long-lasting harm to the relationship between the company and its employees. What does he think will happen between the International Brotherhood of Teamsters and their employees, the organizers? The International states that the executive board at the locals and at the International do not have contractual bargaining agreements giving members the power to keep them in office or vote them out, but organizers are hired, not elected. Therefore, that argument is moot. The two are not the same.

Those who support an at-will status for the union organizers use the same words as any manager at a company regarding the unionization of his or her workforce.

It appears that General President Jimmy Hoffa is willing to test the resolve of the organizers by forcing them into a corner. This is a test to their commitment to fight for a union. If they fail to fight for their own union and contract, how will they be able to stand in front of a worker and tell them to fight? The organizers want due process, according to those involved. If an organizer is not living up to the standards expected of them, then they want a progressive discipline process comparable to what they tell other workers they need. This fight revolves around "at-will employee" versus "just-cause employee."

What about those anti-union organizers? Union members' dues are now paying them to be union-busters. How can they organize nonunion shops, criticizing management for mandatory meetings and a vote-no message, when they themselves engage in the same behavior?

This whole situation begins and ends with General President Hoffa. He could have recognized the organizers without even forcing a vote. Perhaps Hoffa forgot that concept, but he himself advocated for it under EFCA, the Employee Free Choice Act. At the stipulation hearing held by the National Labor Relations Board in Chicago, Hoffa stated he would have recognized the organizers if they had gotten any union but the Teamsters union. Oh, the irony. Perhaps the next company that finds itself under attack from the Teamsters should simply respond that if the Teamsters are not good enough for their own organizers, they are not good enough for that person's employees. Sounds a little bit like Steve Wynn, who, according to Las Vegas lore, swore that he would never have the Teamsters in one of his properties. For the record, there are no Teamsters at Steve Wynn's properties. For all the talk about the war on workers, it seems that the Teamsters union, at least, is selective about which workers you can war against. How in the hell can James Hoffa Jr. stand up in front of a television camera and make the statements he makes when he himself is behaving no differently than corporate America?

When Teamsters Business Agents Formed a Union

This is not an anomaly for the Teamsters; it is standard operating procedure. For example, the secretary-treasurer hires business agents in the locals. At one time, they were elected, and some locals were grandfathered in with those rules, but after changes in the constitution, locals gave the power to hire and fire business agents to the secretary-treasurer. Business agents work with stewards in addressing grievances and contract violations with the employers. They generally are involved with contract negotiations and working with members when issues arise.

In 1997, the business agents at Local 748 organized and formed their own union (Local 748 later merged with two other locals to form Local 948) the National Association of Business Representatives (NABR). Then Teamster General President Ron Carey told them they could not hold dual membership, and they were given Teamsters withdrawal cards. The business agents filed charges with the NLRB to get the Teamsters membership restored. When Jimmy Hoffa Jr. took the reins of the Teamsters, he restored their membership as a part of the settlement with the NLRB regarding the charges that were filed in 1997. On January 1, 2006, a new slate of elected officers took over Local 948. They retained the services of four business agents and terminated the others.

The NABR immediately filed charges with the NLRB against Teamsters Local 948 on behalf of the business agents they represented. The charges filed against Local 948 alleged that the local refused to answer the grievances and did not respond to NABR's request to open contract negotiations until NLRB charges were filed for failure to negotiate in good faith. NABR also filed suit in federal court, and Local 948 followed with a filing of own.

In the meantime, Teamsters Local 948 set about decertifying the NABR. They hired seven new business agents, outnumbering the remaining agents who belonged to the NABR and more than the previous number of agents the former administration had employed. Teamsters Local 948 had its attorney send NABR a decertification letter stating that those business agents did not wish to be represented by NABR.

During this time it was alleged that a Local 948 business agent who had retired was threatened with the loss of his health and welfare if he got involved and helped the NABR. The retiree had earned lifetime benefits after working more than fifteen years for the local.

Many of the union's own members are against their business agents having a collective bargaining agreement. The old paradigm is that when a new executive board takes over, it fires all the holdovers. Many are not rehired. Instead, the new officers hire those who assisted in their election campaign. While the newly elected award their campaign contributors with spoils of victory, qualifications are often absent from the new agents. They are promoted up from the rank and file, and often the only hiring criteria they meet is having been on the winning side.

In locals that have consistently elected the same officers, hence keeping the same business agents, the members appear to have better representation since those in power have the experience and knowledge absent in new administrations. The downside of long-term officers is that, as with politicians, they often lose touch with the members they represent and often take advantage of their position.

The other extreme can be found in Teamsters Local 631. An extremely volatile union even by Teamsters standards, this local seldom has an administration longer than three years, which is the normal term. Because of the high turnover, this local is constantly saddled with inexperienced representation. But paranoia in the union reigns supreme and loyalty is scarce, so most new administrations bring in those they feel they can trust and fire those they cannot, even if they were stellar employees. One can only imagine how the union would view the management of a company that practiced the same concept and fired its workforce every time a new management team was brought in. Of course, no company in its right mind would encourage such a practice, as it would seriously affect the efficiency and productivity of it operations.

Meanwhile, the Office of the Election Supervisor Board investigation into Local 948's officer elections reveals an example of how this political cronyism can manifest itself in the hiring practices of the union. The following is an excerpt from the board's investigation:

> We also credit the statements of Ramírez, Alonzo, Echavarría, and Galván that Herrera stated that she was collecting ballots for the MDSFC slate to insure that her boyfriend, Bob Díaz, might be hired as a business agent for the local union, and find this sufficient proof that Herrera's activity was in support of the MDSFC slate and against the LUS slate. For these reasons, we find that Herrera violated the Rules by interfering with the rights of these members "to independently determine how to cast his/her vote, the right to mark his/her vote in secret and the right to mail the ballot himself/herself." Further, we find that Herrera improperly "encourage[d] IBT member[s]...to give his/her ballot to [her] for marking or mailing," in violation of the Rules. We therefore GRANT the protest with respect to Herrera's conduct and "refer the matter to the Government for appropriate action under law (including the Consent Order)." In making this referral, we note that the misconduct proven here against Herrera strikes at the heart of the democratic reforms instituted under the Consent Decree and must not go unpunished. Moreover, all parties are forewarned that any retaliation undertaken in response to this decision or the action or statement of any witness to expose this wrongdoing will not go unpunished.

On December 4, 2006, an article appeared in the *Modesto Bee* newspaper in which the six terminated business agents accused the new leadership of specifically firing them and then hiring seven new agents with the goal of "union busting" the agents' union. The termination took place on the first day that the newly elected secretary-treasurer's administration took control of the local. Sam Martinez, the newly elected officer, was just doing what all newly elected union officials do in the Teamsters—bringing his political supporters—and he of course denied these allegations. According to the *Modesto Bee:*

> They claim Martinez replaced the six terminated agents with nine supporters, stacking the office in his favor and breaking their union.
>
> "You expect that from a company, but you wouldn't expect that from a union. They are trying to bust a union within a union," said Al Oliver, a longtime business agent who founded the NABR.
>
> David Rosenfeld, the attorney for Local 948, said the agents were replaced so the office could start fresh after last year's election, which boosted Martinez to the union's top post, a three-year position that pays about $87,000 a year.
>
> "The membership of the Local 948 overwhelming selected new officers. Martinez wanted business agents who supported his new ideas and new administration," Rosenfeld said, adding that there were "complaints" about the agents who were let go.
>
> "They can't expect to hold onto their jobs when the leadership has changed through the democratic process," Rosenfeld said.

However, once a union collective bargaining agreement is in place, it is illegal for any employer to hire or fire employees with the intent to "break" the union; just ask Boeing, which only wanted to open a new plant in a right-to-work state.

So did Local 948 violate labor laws? According to one member out of Las Vegas, Ron Roche, an IBT representative and the man Hoffa appointed to assist Local 948's new administration: yes, they did. Mr. Roche apparently used this member as a sounding board in phone conversations as to what method could be used to break the agents' union, with a resulting decertification. After much back-and-forth, both people agreed that the best bet was to hire more agents loyal to the new administration and then have those agents proceed with a decertification, since they would now outnumber the old agents in the union. Acknowledging that charges would be filed, the defense for hiring more agents would be based on the large agricultural base that the local represented, that the hiring of these "seasonal agents" could be reasonably defended because of the uptick in represented employer hiring of seasonal employees during the season. With the plan in place, it was soon acted upon.

The accusations that a union leader would use anti-union tactics on its own employees came at a difficult time for organized labor. Labor was facing tough times, and Local 948 itself had been formed in 2004 when three locals voted to merge to strengthen their leverage and their bottom line in the financial column. By combining Local 748, based in Modesto, with two San Joaquin Valley locals, 94 in Visalia and 746, which had been located in Kingsburg, the locals were able to consolidate and recharge the strength of their bargaining position. Like most businesses during the recession, unions have suffered due to layoffs and plant closures resulting in a decrease in membership and dues. That combined with an abysmal organizing record meant labor unions were faced with a severe downturn in revenue. The three Teamsters locals also suffered as a result of the many food-processing plants moving their operations south of the border into Mexico.

The terminated agents received their bad news when they were called into Sam Martinez's newly acquired office, with the exception of a business agent by the name of Hicks, who received his termination notice by certified letter. Hicks was on disability leave when he received his letter. Oh, the inhumanity of those cold-hearted corporations....oh, wait a minute, that was the union, those fighting for the working man. Hicks had been a business agent from 1995 until his termination in 2004.

Business agents sought security by forming a union and bargaining collectively with their employer, the Teamsters local. Through that agreement, the agents negotiated their wages, pension, and health and welfare benefits, as well as their job security. In an interview with the *Modesto Bee*, another agent stated, "We started talking and thought, 'Why do the members of the cannery have protection, but we don't? Every time a new regime comes, we could get fired.' So we decided, 'Let's organize,'" said Oliver, who retired from Local 748 in 2001.

The practice of awarding political supporters of the elected secretary-treasurer business agents' jobs was a tradition that ended in that local with the formation of the agents' union. Each agent paid an initiation fee of a hundred dollars, with monthly dues set at fifteen dollars per month to go into the newly created NABR. All seven agents joined.

The most important clause in their contract was the one that stipulated they could not be terminated without just cause. That clause is the staple of every union organizer's argument in support of union representation: the fight against at-will status.

Hicks said they believed their union would protect their jobs after elections by stipulating that an agent could not be fired without "just cause." However, according to Chuck Mack, the western regional vice president of the International Brotherhood of Teamsters, a business agent position was never intended to be a lifetime job.

Most union leaders are allowed to choose the business agents, Mack said in an interview with the *Modesto Bee*. "That practice exists so the union membership can remove the head officer and the business agents if they are not doing a good job." I am sure businesses would like the same recourse, Mr. Mack. In fact it appears that most school districts would also like that ability, so why do you think that privilege should only be reserved for your organization?

According to Mr. Mack, the business agents made changes that the membership did not want. Again, should that not be extended to stockholders or parents of children going to schools where some teachers are underperforming?

In the end, though, Chuck Mack and James P. Hoffa won't get involved, as they reportedly stated that the International won't intervene.

This stance was reiterated in a letter responding to terminated business agent Lupe Juarez. In the letter Hoffa stated that the "Teamsters advocate the right for business agents to unionize because it is the same right we advocate for every other worker."

But Hoffa declined to get involved, stating that the Teamsters would not "police the employment practices" at local unions. Wow, talk about lip service. Too bad he did not feel that way about employers he has under union contracts, or perhaps Overnite Trucking Co. Tell me, does the union not police the employment practices of employers or even criticize employers such as Wal-Mart for their employment practices? If they police any employment practices at all, should it not be the ones in their own house?

Like most business agents who leave that position, those who were terminated returned to the positions they had held with employers before accepting the agent positions.

The two charges filed with the NLRB earlier in 2006 against Local 948 claimed that the local violated labor law by attempting to break the union through hiring new agents and by Secretary-Treasurer Sam Martinez's refusal to bargain with them. The claims say Martinez replaced the terminated agents with seasonal business agents to purposefully undermine the business agents' union.

The new agents Martinez hired signed a petition in September, 2006 saying they did not wish to belong to the NABR. Soon afterward, Local 948 said it no longer would recognize the NABR.

David Rosenfeld, the attorney for Local 948, defended the newly hired agents' right to not join the union because they felt it was not representative of the "direction the local was going."

Mr. Rosenfeld, would you have those same feeling about workers in California who are forced to join a union to keep their jobs? Perhaps they feel the union does not represent the "direction" they are going. But then, hypocrisy is the union way, isn't it, Mr. Rosenfeld.

Personally, it is hard for me to believe that any union would condone union busting, especially the International Brotherhood of Teamsters. But the IBT leadership stated that it is a local matter and out of their hands. Ron Rocha had been at the local representing Chuck Mack and Hoffa to ensure a smooth transition. However, International certainly had its hands in this behind the scenes. Rocha was not pleased with the business agents from the old regime and was assisting Herrera with ways to circumvent the business agents' contract. That's when Rocha confided to a former Teamster that they would attempt to break or decertify the union by hiring additional business agents loyal to Herrera.

One of the terminated business agents was offered a position with the International Teamsters. This person had successfully organized Mercer in California—a campaign the IBT had said could not be won. However, there were strings attached to the job offer...go figure. He was asked to withdraw his name from the NABR charges filed with the NLRB and the United States District Court.

He responded by saying, in effect, "How can I be an effective organizer if I do what you are asking me to do? To be a successful organizer, I have to believe in the fundamental right of all workers to organize themselves by forming and/or joining a labor organization of their choice. I would love to be an IBT organizer, but what you are telling me to do goes against that belief. Therefore I will not do what you ask just to be an organizer for the International Brotherhood of Teamsters."

But Local 948 is not alone. Allegedly, Local 705 business agents who were members of the United Mineworkers of America (UMWA) were wrongfully terminated by Steve Pocztowski, then secretary-treasurer of Local 705.

Some members of Local 705 felt that those business agents should have been afforded the same rights as other union members and the ability to enjoy the same privileges, protections, and benefits that the membership had a right to. They did not feel that this was a matter of providing lifetime jobs. They felt that their union representative should have the same job security that they as members enjoyed and if, in fact, they were not performing up to expectations, have the same progressive discipline policies as most covered under a Teamsters contract have.

As much as it may surprise people, unions are among the worst of employers. The Teamsters do not own the market on anti-union practices.

Which again poses the question: are the leaders of unions union-busters?

Chuck Mack was quoted saying that business agents should not be guaranteed lifetime jobs. How does having a union contract guarantee a lifetime job? I would challenge any union official to show a contract their union negotiated that included a guarantee of lifetime employment. If there is such a document, I then encourage all union members to demand that their union representatives give them the same language. In fact, Chuck Mack was spinning the truth to justify breaking a union.

One of the postings on Teamster.net revealed the following:

David Rosenfeld has been practicing law on behalf of the unions since 1973. He is particularly proud of developing creative and unusual tactics, both in the courts as well as outside of the courts. One of the things David likes most about being a union lawyer is the ability to help union officials be more offensive, aggressive and effective. For instance, Teamsters Local 70 has used Rosenfeld's law firm to protect the members' rights under collective bargaining agreements.

IBT Representative Ron Rocha, if we are not mistaken, is also a retired Teamsters Local 70 business agent. He was handpicked by both Hoffa and Mack to be their personal representative at Teamsters Local 948 during the Martinez slate transition period.

Is it coincidence that both Ron Rocha and David Rosenfeld are actively participating in union-busting tactics at Teamsters Local 948?

Is the International Brotherhood of Teamsters General Executive Board supportive of the union-busting tactics? There is circumstantial evidence in support of that belief, including the following.

Campaign Contribution Rules Violation
In another, bigger campaign, the Office of the Election Supervisor Board investigated Teamsters Local 853's questionable fundraising regarding Hoffa's 2006 campaign. The purpose of the investigation revolved around the secretary-treasurer of that local, Rome Aloise, requiring his business agents to give money from their paychecks to the reelection campaign.

Here is an excerpt and the decision from that investigation:

Investigation showed that the Campaign '98 account receives funds from elected officers and full-time business agents of the local union. The bulk of funds contributed to the account are in the form of local union payroll checks issued for vacation pay and made payable to a particular full-time officer or business agent, who then endorses the back of the check and turns it over to Aloise for deposit in the account.

Aloise stated that contributions to the Campaign '98 account are voluntary, but further characterized the contributions by business agents as "job insurance." Aloise elaborated that when a new business agent is hired, he "explain[s] what we do politically and how we do it."

Q: And what do you explain to them?...What do you tell them?

A: That they basically serve at the pleasure of the executive board, and as long as they do their job and the executive board gets re-elected, they're going to have a job. If the executive board does not get re-elected, they may not have a job.

Q: How does that play in with the campaign account?

A: Well, it behooves them to make sure that the current executive board that hired them gets re-elected.

No full-time officer or business agent has declined to contribute to the campaign account.

2.b. Purpose of the Campaign '98 account.

Aloise stated that the purpose of the Campaign '98 account was to collect funds for use in local officer elections:

Q: The purpose of the Campaign '98 account was for local elections, was that correct?

A: That was the reason for its inception and its...continuance.

Aloise testified that he recognized the tremendous need candidates for International office had to raise funds, and he focused on the political benefits that would come to Local Union 853 and to himself from making contributions to a variety of candidates for International office. Accordingly, Aloise stated that he and contributors to the Campaign '98 account discussed using the funds from that account to make campaign contributions to candidates for International office:

"We had discussed the fact that we wanted to spread our contributions around to the various candidates because we thought that politically it was better for the local to do that and frankly better politically for me."

⌒⌒

Q: You said a few minutes ago when you were deciding which candidates to give to that it would be better politically for you guys to spread the contributions around. What did you mean by that?

A: Just what I said. It's better politically for us to do so.

⌒⌒

Q: Tell me what do you mean by that, tell me how it would help you.

A: We are a very political organization as you are well aware and everybody on the national campaign has pressure to raise money. So as in any other political campaign, contributors probably garner more favor than people that don't contribute. So within the politics of our organization there's people that may be influential in one form or another for the local and for our members and for what we do that would be important to the local so spreading it around makes more sense than dumping it into one candidate's fundraising, although ultimately it all goes to the same place as I understand it any way.

Q: Let's talk about that for a second. You said that there's pressure to raise money. What do you mean by pressure to raise money?

A: Well, all the candidates are—have expenses associated with the campaign so there's natural pressure, it's an unpleasant task for any politician to raise money so I'm characterizing it as pressure. Maybe people like to do it. I wouldn't.

Q: Tell me about the process that you went through in deciding... which candidates would get money from the Campaign '98 account when you were spreading it around?

A: I work quite often with many of these—the incumbent candidates in any event and some of them had various divisions, some of them are influential in certain departments. Local 853 is a very diverse, multi-industry local union so we cross almost every department with the exception of UPS and freight, car haul and the International. So there's times where we need assistance from either the division or the department. In some cases that was a consideration. In other cases if they were from the West might make a difference, things of that nature.

Q: So these incumbent candidates, these are the ones that you personally worked with?

A: Yes.

Q: And then did you come up in your mind with a list of who this money was going to go to?

A: Yes.

Q: And then was that communicated to anybody at Local 853?

A: I think I discussed very generally with all of these people that that's what we were going to do.
<end excerpting>

As a result of the investigation, IBT Election Supervisor Richard W. Mark issued the following notice to the local:

NOTICE TO ALL MEMBERS OF LOCAL UNION 853
FROM IBT ELECTION SUPERVISOR RICHARD W.
MARK

The Rules for the 2005–2006 IBT International Union Delegate and International Officer Election ("Rules") permit members to make campaign contributions to any candidate for International office. However, the Rules prohibit use of union funds, personnel and facilities to support any candidate for International office.

The Election Supervisor has found that Rome Aloise and the Executive Board of Local Union 853 violated the Rules by engaging in a scheme to contribute local union funds to candidates for International office. You can read this decision, and the detailed findings at www.ibtvote.org. Specifically, the Election Supervisor has found that the Executive Board, on a motion made by Aloise, increased the vacation entitlement for all full-time officers and full-time business agents of the local union by one week per year so that those persons would in turn donate the pay for that additional week of vacation to a fund to be used to make campaign contributions to candidates for International office. Accordingly, the Election Supervisor has found that the increase in vacation was a sham to conceal improper union contributions to candidates.

The Election Supervisor has found that individuals who made campaign contributions were reimbursed from the pooled account and that this concealed the true source of the reported contributions and violated the Rules that require campaign contributions to be made for the International officer election and attributed exclusively to eligible members.

The Election Supervisor has found that the campaign account into which the vacation paychecks were deposited was maintained by local union personnel using local union facilities.

The Election Supervisor will not tolerate such improper use of union funds, personnel and facilities.

Accordingly, the Election Supervisor has ordered the improper contributions to be returned to the local union treasury and the additional week of vacation entitlement the Executive Board ordered to be revoked from the vacation schedule, retroactive to the date the schedule was increased.

The Election Supervisor has also ordered this notice to be mailed to all members of Local Union 853, posted on all union bulletin boards under the local union's jurisdiction for a period through November 14, 2006.

And that in a nutshell is the Teamsters' version of a democracy and of representation elected by the members. Business agents are very much at the mercy of the election results even though they are hired and not elected. Could you imagine what the union's response would be if an employer wanted a clause in the contract stating that every time managers were replaced, the new managers were free to terminate all workers in that department and replace them with their own people. I doubt any union would agree to that. In fact, I'm sure Hoffa would scream foul into the nearest microphone he could find.

Ohio Local Won't Negotiate with Office Workers

Across the country, in Youngstown, Ohio, on August 18, 2010, Grace Wyler wrote the following headline:

Teamster leaders accused of unfair practices

What caused such a headline to appear in the Youngstown newspaper? Well it seems that Teamsters Local 377 had decided to play the character of bad employer and was now on the receiving end of charges claiming that the officials of the local were engaging in unfair labor practices against its own employees. Two employees had fanned the embers of political unrest at Local 377, unrest that has been the standard operating procedure for the local for many years.

Like many unions, Local 377 has its share of infighting, and the latest charges brought by the two employees, Denise Sculli and former receptionist Michelle Sinkele, just added more fuel to the blaze. Sculli, the current office manager, and Sinkele had been entangled in a contract dispute since March 2010 with the local's elected officials. According to the article in the Youngstown paper:

*Sinkele was laid off temporarily in June for "economic reasons,"
union officials said. The two women, members of the Professional Office Workers union, recently filed charges against the Teamsters with
the National Labor Relations Board. The claims accuse Teamsters officials of refusing to negotiate any renewal or extension of their contract, which expired in March, and of violating the terms of their
collective-bargaining agreement.*

The charges also state the Teamsters improperly laid off Sinkele.

After more than two decades of successful contract negotiations with the Professional Office Workers, John Lesicko, the local's
secretary-treasurer, confirmed that the local would not be renewing
the contract with the office workers. Who would have thought it was
that easy? So the next time a company decides that, gee, these union
contracts are just too much of a pain in the ass, we just won't renew
them, I am sure the unions will understand. After all, we should all
practice what we preach, right guys? Isn't the purpose of union contracts and negotiations supposed to be about protecting workers'
rights, protecting the company, and both sides meeting in the middle
to find an agreement? Obviously not at Local 377 in Youngstown,
Ohio.

Again, the newly elected officials had "issues" with the language
in the contract negotiated by a previous administration, and the
workers paid the price. Of course, Mr. Lesicko never provided anyone with the language the local found offensive in the contract and
like any good union official would say, these attacks against him and
the new administration were totally unfounded and totally politically
motivated. I mean, like totally.

Are Teamsters Union-busters?

Based on the facts provided here, I am of the opinion that in
the above example, as well as the previously mentioned Modesto and
Chicago examples, the employer (union local) did, in fact, union bust.

Slowly but surely the evidence is starting to mount that the answer to the question—are Teamsters union-busters?—is a resounding
yes.

Take for example, the Teamsters' style in the art of negotiating with their own unionized employees. The following is a letter sent out to employees of the Teamsters Local 631 Training Trust Facility.

Professional Clerical and Miscellaneous Employees Local Union 995

Mike Magnani, Secretary-Treasurer   Helen Green, President

300 SHADOW LANE • (702) 385-0995 • Fax (702) 385-4410 • LAS VEGAS, NEVADA 89106

TO: **All Teamsters Local 995 Members Employed At The Teamsters Local 631 Construction And Convention Training Trust Facility**

FROM: **Mike Magnani, Secretary-Treasurer**

Subject: **Important Notice**

Important

As you are aware, a contract ratification and strike vote took place on Saturday, August 11, 2007. Not too long after that meeting took place, one of our meeting participants contacted me to advise that he received what he perceived as a threatening phone call from a trustee. That individual saved that message on his phone and sent me a statement of specifics concerning that message.

Should anyone else receive an implied or direct threat from any of the Trust Trustees or Local Union leaders, I would ask that you record the date, time, place, who contacted you, how you were contacted, whether there are witnesses and, specifically, what was said or done.

Remember, your employer is not supposed to deal with our members directly concerning contract negotiations. They are required to deal with your Union representative. I am therefore asking our members employed at this facility not to have any conversation with any of the Trust fund or Teamsters Local 631 leadership concerning contract negotiations. Tell those folks to respectfully direct those questions or comments to me. That action should save us all some grief.

Thank you.

(Mailed 8/14/07)

AFFILIATED WITH THE INTERNATIONAL BROTHERHOOD OF TEAMSTERS, AFL-CIO

In this case, members of Teamsters Local 995 worked for Teamsters 631 Training Trust as instructors, providing trade training. When negotiations stalled, the secretary-treasurer of Local 631, Wayne King Sr., decided to handle negotiations in the way most associated with union thuggery: threats and coercion. The following article appeared in the *Las Vegas Sun*:

> *Teamsters' next hurdle: Election*
> *Accusations already flying over contested contract by J. Patrick Coolican and Michael Mishak on Saturday, April 5, 2008. The following is an excerpt from that article...*
> *Last year King was negotiating with members of a different local, Teamsters 995, who worked in a training facility owned by Local 631. King demanded they accept at-will employment, allowing Local 631 to fire the 995 workers whenever it pleased and for whatever reason.*
> *As a bargaining tool for a union, it was counterintuitive; the whole point of unions is to give workers rights in the face of management that would prefer to grant none. King sought to curtail the rights of those workers.*

The negotiations started in November 2006, with the contract expiring in December of that same year. King was placed in his position as the secretary-treasurer when the Internal Review Board, the Department of Justice oversight that had been placed inside the Teamsters as a condition of the Consent Decree (see appendix), removed Edmund Burke for bringing reproach upon the union. Negotiations became contentious.

In January 2007, King failed to extend the current contract until a new agreement was reached. This led to a suspension of health insurance and pension contributions. According to an employee of Southwest Administrators in Las Vegas, the company that administered the training-trust funds and was responsible for recording the minutes to the training trust's executive board meetings, King did this to pressure the employees into a substandard agreement. The negotiations became hostile, and in June 2007 Teamsters 631 Training Trust fired the director, who was also the steward and lead negotiator for the employees and the administrative assistant.

A subsequent hearing was held between Mike Magnani, secretary-treasurer for Local 995, which represented the employees, and Wayne King, secretary-treasurer of Local 631. The clash between the two men came as Mike Magnani attempted to represent one of the terminated workers. According to a recording made by one of the meeting attendees, the hearing culminated in a profanity-laden shouting match when King was questioned over utilizing intimidation as a tactic to put pressure on the employee. King, with all the pomposity of...well, of a king, refused to answer the query about his tactics. The following was recorded and then printed in the *Las Vegas Sun* newspaper:

> *Magnani: You know what? You're an #$@!*
> *King: Yes I am.*
> *Magnani: You're an #$@!*
> *King: You don't come in here and accuse me of doing stuff like that. Kiss my #@$.*

Although Local 995 officials refused to respond to requests from the local press about the incident, in an article in the *Las Vegas Sun*, Wayne King's right-hand man, Tommy Blitsch, questioned the authenticity of the meeting minutes—like any good water boy hauling the water of the secretary-treasurer. Just for the record, the *Sun* reporters stated that they had heard the recording and authenticated the minutes with more than one person present at the meeting, and I acquired a copy of the minutes of the meeting and the tape and listened to it myself.

The following is the complete transcript from the recording of that meeting:

> *Board Meeting August 8, 2007. Denise Malwitz concerning grievance on termination.*
> *Wayne King: Before we get started I would ask everyone to give their name. Wayne King Secretary Treasurer 631.*
> *Vince Dickenson, Freeman*
> *Don Mc Namee, Vice President 631*
> *Maurice Peoples, South West Administrators*

Mike Shea, South West Administrators
Martin Laurel, GES
Kathy, Office Administrator 995
Mike Magnani, Secretary Treasurer 995
Denise Malwitz
unknown
Joe Kaplin, Lawyer
Elaina Youchau, Lawyer
Tommy Blitch, President 631

Mike (995): The notice I received from you dated July 10th, 2007, from Mike Shea basically says the purpose of this hearing of circumstances leading to their termination. So in order for us to adequately continue and explain our actions we have to know what that means. Can somebody tell us what that means?

Wayne (631): We're here, we're here for her to address the board with any concerns she has over her termination. That's all I know.

Mike (995): O.K. I'm just telling you it's hard for us to defend ourselves or tell you why we think you erred if we don't know why you took the action you've taken and to date nobody has said anything to her, wait, let me just run something by you. I think you've put us in an awkward position where by there is absolutely no defense for nothing. You can't defend yourself if you don't know what the issue is. I hate to say it with all of you here. It's like a sham meeting there's no sense in having a meeting if you want us to get our—our knees and beg because that's the only opportunity we have so let me just run some things by you. It makes no sense to defend ourselves if we don't know what we're defending. I don't know, we ate the wrong thing for lunch yesterday. I don't know and you aren't willing to tell us so let's go this way. Denise has advised me that some things, some awkward things have been happening lately. Stuff like people have been accessing her computer from remotely and listening to a lot of stuff and watching her e-mails. Cars parked in front of her house. I don't know whether you have anything to do with it or not.

I would hope you don't. I hope you wouldn't go that far but I can tell you that one more incident will have police involvement.

Wayne (631): Let's stop there.
Mike (995): Wait.
Wayne (631): Naw let's stop right there.
Mike (995): No.

Wayne (631): Let's stop right there we are not involved.

Mike (995): You can do what you want but I have the floor right now. You'll wait until I'm done.

Wayne (631): No. No. The meeting is over.

Mike (995): Go to Hell.

Wayne (631): Your God damn right it is. Get your ass out of here.

Mike (995): Fuck you.

Wayne (631): O.K. Suck my dick.

Mike (995): You know what why don't you come over here, I'll give you some of it.

Wayne (631): You want to use your mouth for something.

Mike (995): You know what you're an asshole.

Wayne (631): Yes I am.

Mike (995): You don't treat people like that. You're an asshole.

Wayne (631): You don't come in here and accuse me of doing stuff like that. Kiss my ass.

Mike (995): You don't tell me when I'm in here representing someone.

Wayne (631): You're done.

Mike (995): Then tell me half way through representation.

Wayne (631): You're done.

Mike (995): No I'm not done. You don't tell me to shut up.

Wayne (631): Yeah you are.

Mike (995): You haven't seen the last of me.

Wayne (631): You're done here.

Mike (995): I'm not done you haven't seen the last of me.

At that point I left the room because I was afraid there was going to be a fight. They continued to exchange words after I left.

Teamsters Inc.: Strikebreakers

Another example of Teamsters Inc. was when the Teamsters encountered a stone wall while negotiating with employees at the marble palace. The employees were represented by the Office Professional Employees International Union (OPEIU) during 2009. OPEIU, which represented many of the administrative support staff, began representing the Teamsters office staff during Ron Carey's reign as general president and had since negotiated two contracts under Hoffa. In an interesting intra-union political twist, OPEIU was still affiliated with the AFL-CIO, while Hoffa had since joined the SEIU in breaking away from the old-guard establishment.

The problems started when the Teamsters (like most business-es these days) found themselves struggling financially and decided to take a hard line at the bargaining table—resulting in the threat of a strike against the Teamsters by their own employees. A series of letters sent out in July threatened layoffs in mid-September. The following letter, sent out to all principle officers at the International and its locals, could easily be confused with one from a corporation.

INTERNATIONAL BROTHERHOOD of TEAMSTERS

JAMES P. HOFFA
General President

25 Louisiana Avenue, NW
Washington, DC 20001

C. THOMAS KEEGEL
General Secretary-Treasurer

202.624.6800
www.teamster.org

July 29, 2009

Dear Principal Officer:

We are writing to update you on the negotiations that are currently taking place with the union covering the IBT's building workforce. Unfortunately the negotiations are not going well.

All unionized workers at the IBT's Headquarters are a valuable part of our team and provide important services to Teamster members and our affiliate Locals. However, their union at the bargaining table refuses to acknowledge the current economic conditions and the impact on per capita revenues at the IBT. As you are well aware, Local Union affiliates are also feeling the pinch and we certainly recognize that the operations of the IBT rely on per capita payments calculated on membership dues.

The bargaining unit at the IBT was organized during the Carey years as building workers sought to protect themselves through representation by another union. Since 1998, when we took office, we successfully negotiated two collective bargaining agreements with terms that shared the improving financial condition at the IBT with those workers. We are now asking that workers share in the prudent belt-tightening.

As in any negotiations, these union members have a right to take strike action and their union knows the embarrassment that such an event would create for the IBT. However, no amount of embarrassment will cause us to commit to a collective bargaining agreement that jeopardizes the financial health of your International Union.

Though it pains us to do so, we must make contingency plans to operate in the event of a labor dispute.

In closing, we commit to our Locals that we will stay at the bargaining table as long as it takes in these difficult times. We will be considerate in the negotiations to our IBT employees and will remain true to the principles that our union stands for.

Fraternally,

James P. Hoffa
General President

C. Thomas Keegel
General Secretary-Treasurer

This potentially embarrassing situation did nothing to sway Hoffa and his secretary-treasurer, Tom Keegel, from their course as the union braced itself for a very public strike. In August 2009, Ed Keyser, Hoffa's administrative assistant sent a memo to all department heads at International instructing them to prepare a departmental operating plan for each department to follow if they had to work behind the picket lines.

As every union member knows, anyone who works behind a picket line is a scab. In fact, the union definition of scab is as follows: "A scab is a person who refuses to join a union; crosses or works behind a strike line in an attempt by the employer to break the strike; strikebreakers." So we have already ascertained that the Teamsters engage in union busting, but do they engage in strikebreaking?

According to the following letter, that is exactly what they do. Again, the hypocrisy of the union comes out in a blatant memo they themselves wrote, showing they have the audacity to engage in the same practices that they themselves condemn corporate America for. As for a scabbing, well Hoffa did refuse to honor the mechanics' strike line against Northwest Airlines; hell, he even flew on Northwest during the strike to his home in Detroit and never once instructed the travel department to stop booking on Northwest. If I were US Airways, I would be crying foul and disparity of treatment!

MEMORANDUM

To: Department/Division Directors

From: Edward F. Keyser, Jr., Administrative Assistant to the General President

Date: August 25, 2009

Re: Contingency Plans

This is to request that you submit to me, no later than 9 a.m. tomorrow (Wednesday, August 26, 2009), a contingency plan. Please specify how you plan to conduct your department's/division's business in the event that your staff is not allowed to enter the building due to strike action taken by OPEIU Local 2.

Thank you for your cooperation in this matter. Please be sure to copy Leo Deaner on your correspondence. Should you have any questions, I can be reached at: (202) 624-8750.

EFK/sg

cc: Leo Deaner, Executive Assistant to the General President
      Richard C. Bell, Executive Assistant to the General Secretary-Treasurer

September 1, 2009: The Hoffa administration continued to threaten employees working at the Teamsters headquarters who were bargaining to try to avoid concessions for the first time in the two decades they had been negotiating a contract. These employees included janitors, secretaries, and other support staff in all the International's departments.

Like their corporate counterparts, whom Hoffa and his union army accuse of greed at their workers' expense, Hoffa and Keegel each had had large raises two years prior to the negotiations in the form of an oversized "housing allowance" and had no plans to cut their own salary in the face of the this "economic belt tightening." No, they felt above the equality of sacrifice that they preach to corporate America.

Under Hoffa, the executive staff had increased, and as a result, multiple salaries paid by the International increased ten times over what they were.

These high-and-mighty union officials have special pensions that provide for a millionaire's lifestyle upon retirement. When traveling, International officials get a meal allowance of $100 per day. And yet they are steadfast in insisting that their own staff employees need to sacrifice.

The fact is that if any other company had offered the same contract that the IBT put forth to its workers, there would have been all hell to pay as far as workers' rights! In fact, a clause was added called a Zipper Clause. Now pay attention corporate America. A Zipper Clause is a clause that the International Brotherhood of Teamsters would not be obligated to bargain or negotiate with respect to any matter referred to in the contract—Which means that IBT could legally refuse to bargain over any issue during the life of the contract. Very cool. And you thought you could learn nothing about labor relations from the union surprise surprise. If the thought that SEIU and the Teamsters were more than just "friends" crossed anyone's mind , then this should more than reinforce that thought. While the Teamsters were engaged in a battle with their own employees a mirror image of their conflict was being played out by SEIU. According to unfair labor practice charges filed by SEIU employees, SEIU was accused of laying off their own unionized employees and replacing them with contract workers in order to undermine the union that represented them.

While these stories are tremendously sardonic, they also expose union leaders for what they are—as bottom-line oriented as the corporate CEOs they repeatedly demonize.

For the Teamsters, union busting seemed to be a very successful endeavor; however, their celebration was short-lived. Through the confusion that ensued, an election date was actually set for the Teamsters organizers. It seemed that FAIR did not withdraw its petition, and a mail-in ballot was established as the voting method. On May 29, 2012, the NLRB set the deadline for mail-in ballots for the vote on whether these employees would be represented by FAIR.

A few weeks before the deadline, the following letter went out to all the organizers:

What is happening here?

Being disrespectful and making fun of your coworkers that do not agree with your stance is not the way to win friends and influence people. It is a direct reflection of those that are leading the FAIR campaign and the FAIR organization itself.
We should all know this is no way to build a union or a strong bargaining unit.

Many questions have been asked of FAIR and their supporters that directly deal with our jobs and futures with no answers. All that has been handed back is "I want"...... fill in the blank, calling coworkers names, ignoring the question asked and then making fun of the person asking.
Is that how we do it?

This chosen theme of not discussing, non inclusion, belittling, no plan for success and not answering real questions that have real consequences is a very good reason to make the choice not to support the FAIR agenda.

You will make one of the most important decisions of your Teamster career in the upcoming representational election. Please ask yourself the following questions.

Will Teamster Locals allow FAIR organizers to perform work in their house?

Are you willing to betray the faith and respect given you by Teamster leaders?

Are you willing to put what you currently have on the table?

How will FAIR get you a contract?
Are you willing to break the oath that you took to the Teamsters?

Was putting the FAIR agenda out to Teamster locals and Principal Officers a good idea?

The Proud Teamsters below hold a deep-seated belief in the Teamsters Union as we believe our coworkers do also. The Proud Teamsters listed believe our appointment to serve at the pleasure of the General President as a Teamster Organizer is a privilege, an honor and reflects our strong devotion to the Teamster membership. We serve our Teamster administration and members proudly.

We believe support and protection of our great Teamsters Union is without fail and has become a way of life for all Teamster Organizers. Compliance with our Teamster constitution is a cherished and fundamental duty that every Teamster swears allegiance too and takes very seriously.

We want to stay Teamsters. It is not our desire to be a part of another organization. We want to make it very clear that we choose to remain Teamster members.

We are Proud Teamsters Staying Teamsters

Jim Leonhardt	Fuad Osman
Joel Wood	Dean Phinney
Michael Giovannetti	Greg Chockley
Michael Marvray	Jim Kellepourey
Stephen Hanson	Ricardo Hidalgo
Sean O'Neill	Jason Gately
Michele Goodman	Walter Westfield
Bob Maldunas	James Curbeam
Tremayne Johnson	
Terry Stark	

With all of this being said;
We do hear our brothers and sisters crying out to be heard.
We do agree that obviously issues exist or you would not have reacted this way, your concerns should be addressed.
We do not believe that bringing in an outside organization is the answer nor will bringing in a competing organization end well for any of us.

We have delivered great victories together and should not end in a great defeat. If items need to be addressed, we need to be the ones to address them in our house.

We believe we all should talk as Teamsters, to each other as Teamsters and work it out as Teamsters.

WE all need to work together.

For anyone who is or has been involved in a union campaign, you would recognize this tactic normally utilized by employees and "union-busters" involved in a union-avoidance campaign after an employee group had filed for representation from a union. The above correspondence came from an entity called a vote-no committee. The committee is formed by employees who do not wish to have a union in the workplace. They are often ostracized by the union and personally attacked as being scabs, rats, union-busters, and employer lackeys.

The battle also played out among the rank-and-file members. Those who supported the anti-union campaign being waged at the international level felt that those hired as organizers knew the inherent risk of their at-will employment and should just go away quietly when they were terminated. One can only wonder if those rank-and-file members feel the same way about their employment with their employers. Or what about those people who accept employment with a company knowing it is nonunion and either at-will employment or employment based on a laid-out set of in-house progressive discipline policies?. Would they say that those who want to bring a union into their place of employment knew what they were getting into? That they should just leave their place of employment and go away quietly?

Union supporters often fire back with their own flyers and mail-outs, and the Teamsters employees were no different.

Listed below are active Teamsters employed as in-house union-busters. This is a letter sent out to pro-union organizers. Enjoy!

If they show up at your local, let your voice be heard.

The Proud Anti-Union Teamsters listed below hold a deep-seated belief in
the demise of the Teamsters Union and are committed to the destruction of Union values.
The Proud Anti-Union Teamsters listed believe our appointment to serve at the pleasure and of the
General President as a internal Union Buster is a privilege, an honor, and reflects our strong devotion to
the Management at the costly expense of the Teamster membership. We serve our Teamster Masters proudly.

Support and protection of our overly inflated paycheck is
without fail and has become a way of life for all Anti-Union organizers.
Compliance with our Teamster constitution has been ignored although it is our
fundamental duty that every Teamster swears allegiance to and should
take very seriously depending on their pay scale or who's ass they have to lick.

We want to stay Anti-Union Teamsters. It is not our desire to be a part of
another organization. We want to make it very clear that we
choose to remain Anti-Union Teamster. Because more damage can be accomplished from the inside
under the cloak of the organizing department.

We are Proud Anti-Union Teamsters Staying Anti-Union Teamsters

Jim Leonhardt	Fuad Osman
Joel Wood	Dean Phinney
Michael Giovannetti	Greg Chockley
Michael Marvray	Jim Kellepourey
Stephen Hanson	Ricardo Hidalgo
Sean O'Neill	Jason Gately
Michele Goodman	Walter Westfield
Bob Maldunas	James Curbeam
Tremayne Johnson	Terry Stark

With all of this being said;
We do hear our brothers and sisters crying out to be heard because they don't make as much as us.
We do understand and it's a shame you couldn't find someone's balls to nestle under.
We do agree that obviously issues exist or you would not have reacted in
such a manner. Unfortunately, you have decided stand for what you believe in instead of taking payment to destroy the Teamsters Union. Your concerns will continue to be ignored.
We do not believe that bringing in an outside organization is the answer, because there is a real chance that we will have to all be treated and paid fairly.
Nor will bringing in an outside organization end well for any of you.
We have delivered great victories together while taking sole credit, and should not end in a great defeat.
What the membership doesn't know will not hurt them.
If items need to be addressed, we need to be the ones to sweep them under the rug and ignore them.
We believe we all should talk as two faced Union Busters, to each other as
Teamsters and work it out as Management sees fit.
WE can do this, if YOU just do as you're told.
Speaking up and demanding respect and dignity is a commodity that is highly over rated.
Come on, get on board. Together we have an opportunity to rape this Union from the inside out using the Proud Anti-Union Teamsters banner that has already been
approved by Jack, Manny, and Jeff.

Protect YOUR paycheck, not your rights.

The other half of the rank and file were firmly on the side of the
organizers' right to union representation. Some felt that the entire
IBT internal organizer employment policies were wrong, including

the policies that only allow "field organizers" to be employed by the IBT for four years. Once organizers approach that time, they are told their services are no longer needed. Some field organizers are let go before the four-year mark because of internal politics or because they push back on the "management" level of the international union. The organizing department is notorious for firing field organizers who do not fit in with the department's social environment. They are pulled from their crafts with no recall rights, only to be fired when the "powers that be" have no use for them. Every employer that would think of acting this way with its employees would find a public-relations nightmare on its doorstep as the union publicly flogged them for those very same actions.

Some members, in fact, feel that the organizers were used as nothing more than political pawns to quiet down the membership, to take heat off when members complained about the organizing department not organizing enough. Rank-and-file members ask that if the organizing department is so proud of being Teamsters, why do they keep hiring from outside the organization? According to West Coast members, the West Coast organizing director has hired from the LA Federal Credit Union, from LAANE, from Wells Fargo Bank...and the list goes on.

However, it is important to realize that as Jimmy Hoffa Jr. stated prior to the Teamsters Unity Conference in Las Vegas, Nevada, in May 2012, that the International's official stance was one of neutrality. Funny about that stance, because if the big guy really believed in what he preached, he would have acknowledged the union the minute a majority of the cards were signed. Card check anyone? Perhaps he would have recognized it had it been called EFCA, or Employee Free Choice Act. Perhaps his announcement of neutrality came on the heels of hearing that the organizers planned a rally of their at the Unity Conference. Guess it might be a bit embarrassing to be at your own Unity Conference and have your employees' own employees publicly saying, "not feeling the love, Hoffa."

On May 30, 2012, the Teamsters organizers announced that they had won, by a two-vote margin, their right to be represented.

The count was eighteen for the union and sixteen against—only thirty-four people, but the fight had been won.

While most would wonder at the fact that the International Brotherhood of Teamsters only had about forty organizers, everyone should remember that the union has perfected the art of remaining union-free for its own employees. Most are temporary or project organizers with defined start and end dates. Those employees or organizers are not eligible to vote or be represented under the National Labor Relations Act. Why do you think the Teamsters and other unions do that? Employers and companies could learn from the example the unions set. Unions are not really all that pro-worker after all.

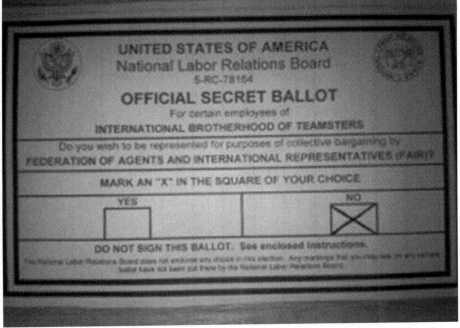

NOTICE TO ALL MEMBERS OF LOCAL UNION 853

In July the following letter was sent to President Hoffa from the newly organized organizers.

July 19, 2012

Dear General President Hoffa and General Executive Board,

We would like to take a moment address you concerning the result of our organizing efforts. As you are aware, originally the International Organizers sought representation through card check recognition with a Teamsters local. The rationale was that we were all dues paying Teamsters and wanted to expand our rights to collective bargaining in house. At that time we were instructed by your legal team that it would create a conflict of interest and we should seek representation from another entity in order to avoid any legal dilemma. We complied with those instructions sought representation, filed for and prevailed in an election with the NLRB. What is troublesome is the ongoing conduct of the senior staff of this organizing department. We succeeded in the election, like tens of thousands of workers across this country do every year. The continuing barrage of frivolous objections and appeals by our senior staff in order to stall and delay the exercise of our rights is appalling. This is a carbon copy of the behavior engaged in the ongoing war on workers.

The use of Teamster member's dues including yours and ours, to employ union busting tactics is not approved of by our membership or the labor movement at large. This shameful behavior is hypocritical to say the least. Every day we lobby communities, politicians, and our constituents for card check recognition, neutrality and for fair expedited bargaining. At every juncture to date, this department has denied us these precepts and involved itself in the same unethical behavior as those employers we combat daily. We are simply asking to move forward in the manner that befits the process, our members, and the labor movement. Brother Hoffa you are the face of labor in this country, and the leading advocate for workers both organized and unorganized. It makes us proud to engage these workers daily and tell them the Teamsters and Jim Hoffa has your back. It inspires them in their need to obtain collective bargaining for themselves and their families. As we all know, a represented workforce better serves both employee and employer in creating workplace fairness and justice. This arrangement creates a more productive outcome for all parties involved. We are now and always have been ardent supporters of the Hoffa GEB and administration. We have contributed both monetarily and donated countless hours of our off time in support of this administration. These actions were taken in the knowledge and belief that our great union and its membership are best served by your leadership. We are ready to begin negotiating a collective bargaining agreement that will create a more positive workplace allowing us to serve our brothers and sisters, the Teamster membership.

In Solidarity,

The Steering Committee of the Teamster Staff Organizers (FAIR)

Chapter 2
SEIU Union Busting Its Own Members

"And, you know, what really matters is what do the leaders of organizations do about changing the lives of the people, you know, who are—get up every day and help build the organization."
—Andy Stern, former SEIU president, in an interview with NPR, April 15, 2010

FORM EXEMPT UNDER 44 U.S.C 3512

FORM NLRB-501 (2-08)	UNITED STATES OF AMERICA NATIONAL LABOR RELATIONS BOARD CHARGE AGAINST EMPLOYER	DO NOT WRITE IN THIS SPACE	
	NLRB REGION 32	Case 32-CA-25781	Date Filed 7/1/2011

INSTRUCTIONS:
File an original with NLRB Regional Director for the region in which the alleged unfair labor practice occurred or is occurring.

1. EMPLOYER AGAINST WHOM CHARGE IS BROUGHT

a. Name of Employer SEIU UHW		OAKLAND, CA		b. Tel. No. (510)251-1250
				c. Cell No. ( ) -
				f. Fax No. (510)763-2680
d. Address (Street, city, state, and ZIP code) 560 Thomas L Berkley Way		e. Employer Representative Myriam Escamilla		g. e-Mail mescamilla@seiu-uhw.org
Oakland	CA 94612-			h. Number of workers employed 200 - 300
i. Type of Establishment (factory, mine, wholesaler, etc.) labor organization		j. Identify principal product or service labor organization		

k. The above-named employer has engaged in and is engaging in unfair labor practices within the meaning of section 8(a), subsections (1) and (list subsections) _____ of the National Labor Relations Act, and these unfair labor practices are practices affecting commerce within the meaning of the Act, or these unfair labor practices are unfair practices affecting commerce within the meaning of the Act and the Postal Reorganization Act.

2. Basis of the Charge (set forth a clear and concise statement of the facts constituting the alleged unfair labor practices)

1. On or about March 18, 2011, the above-named Employer, through its agent, officer, and representative Susie Miranda, threatened organizer/representative Saliem Aregaye with unspecified reprisals because Aregaye engaged in protected concerted activity; i.e. organizing co-workers to file charges with the NLRB and to address working conditions.

2. On or about April 5, 2011, the above-named Employer issued a poor, false and misleading work review to Saliem Aregaye in retaliation for Aregaye's protected concerted activity. See above definition of protected concerted activity in paragraph 1.

3. On or about May 13, 2011, the above-named Employer terminated Saliem Aregaye in retaliation for Aregaye's protected concerted activity. See above definition of protected concerted activity in paragraph 1.

COPY SENT NLRB

3. Full name of party filing charge (if labor organization, give full name, including local name and number) _____ By _____		
Saliem Tekeste Aregaye		
4a. Address (Street and number, city, state, and ZIP code) Apt. # 1		4a. Tel. No. _____
		4b. Cell No. _____
San Diego	CA 92111-	4d. Fax No. ( ) -
		4e. e-Mail _____@yahoo.com

5. Full name of national or international labor organization of which it is an affiliate or constituent unit (to be filled in when charge is filed by a labor organization)

6. DECLARATION		Tel. No. _____
I declare that I have read the above charge and that the statements are true to the best of my knowledge and belief.		
By _____ (signature of representative or person making charge)	Saliem Aregaye, Individual (Print/type name and title or office, if any)	Office, if any, Cell No. _____
		Fax No. ( ) -
Saliem Tekeste Aregaye Apt. #1		e-Mail _____@yahoo.com
Address San Diego CA 9211-1	06/30/11 (date)	

WILLFUL FALSE STATEMENTS ON THIS CHARGE CAN BE PUNISHED BY FINE AND IMPRISONMENT (U.S. CODE, TITLE 18, SECTION 1001)

PRIVACY ACT STATEMENT   21-2011-1545

Solicitation of the information on this form is authorized by the National Labor Relations Act (NLRA), 29 U.S.C. § 151 et seq. The principal use of the information is to assist the National Labor Relations Board (NLRB) in processing unfair labor practice and related proceedings or litigation. The routine uses for the information are fully set forth in the Federal Register, 71 Fed. Reg. 74942-43 (Dec. 13, 2006). The NLRB will further explain these uses upon request. Disclosure of this information to the NLRB is voluntary; however, failure to supply the information will cause the NLRB to decline to invoke its processes.

Union organizers have a tough job. They must be able to take rejection, be willing to stay away from their families for extended periods, and have the ability to babysit adults through an emotionally charged period in their lives. They receive no admiration from their unions, which work them like dogs, and the companies they seek to organize treat them like lepers. To paraphrase a Rodney Dangerfield joke, "They get no respect."

Therefore, it is not surprising that more and more organizers seek the same fantasy world they promise their prospective members. A world where they receive respect from their employers, have a voice in the work place, and have job security—which seems to elude most employees of unions.

Rumors in the organizing world point the finger at the Service Employees International Union as one of the worst unions to work for as an organizer. Overshadowed by internal politics and backstabbing, with an underlying need to increase dues more than guarantee a good contract, SEIU has become the bad boy of the union world. Once upon a time, the Teamsters held the honor of being the union most likely to inject violence into their actions, but they have been far outpaced by SEIU's willingness to use and abuse any and all that get in the way of the organization's agenda. And not only companies, but also other unions. Their fight is more of a far-left political fight than any fight for workers' rights.

Like the Teamsters, SEIU does not believe that their own employees have the same rights to organize that they bully companies into accepting.

According to all reports and to Hamilton Gramajo himself, Gramajo worked as an SEIU organizer seven days a week. His days were long, often over sixteen hours, without even time off for church on Sunday mornings. When he expressed his frustration with his work schedule to his union bosses, his complaints fell on deaf ears. After all, he should be lucky he had a job—and not just any job, but a noble job for a cause that he should happily sacrifice for.

Hamilton was working on the SEIU campaign Justice for Janitors in 2006 when the stress of trying to organize 5,300 janitors, as well as dealing with pressure from union bigwigs to keep his numbers up, resulted in a decline in his physical well-being. As a result of his anxiety and excessive hours at work, Hamilton started experiencing chest pains. He realized he was telling the workers that they should not have to put up with long hours and having their rights trampled, at the same time that he was allowing those same issues to be a part of his work life.

Gramajo and other SEIU organizers did for themselves what they had done for other workers. They organized themselves. They selected FAIR as their union representative. Through FAIR they asked for better working conditions, including limited time away from home and no longer having to eat their meals in their cars, as well as job security. Funny how job security keeps coming up time after time for workers employed by unions, isn't it? While the Justice for Janitors campaign ended with SEIU signing contracts with five Houston-based janitorial companies, the SEIU organizers were not as lucky.

Unhappy with their organizers for having the boldness to join a union themselves, SEIU retaliated fast and hard. The union would not tolerate the idea of an internal organizing drive happening among their own workforce. Some organizers were just terminated outright, while others were assigned to difficult campaigns in various locations to keep them separate from the others. Hamilton Gramajo was terminated. After all, the union would not accept that which they pushed onto corporate America.

The resulting battle that pitted SEIU against its own organizers ended up with multiple charges being filed with the National Labor Relations Board. Charges ranged from work-rule violations by the union, allegations that SEIU refused to communicate or follow seniority layoff and recall protocols, and termination of employees for exercising their right to participate in protected union activity.

SEIU contends that they willingly recognized the union, but that FAIR that failed in its obligations to the employees it represents. Instead of following the grievance procedure, FAIR has been filing charges of unfair labor practices with the NLRB. These practices, according to FAIR, included reducing pay and failing to grant sick time and vacation leave. According to Norm Yen, SEIU Texas state director, there was no reasoning with the FAIR representative. The case ended up in arbitration.

This isn't the first time that SEIU has run into trouble with its own employees.

HOPE—the Houston Organization of Public Employees, which was formed when SEIU and the American Federation of State, County, and Municipal Employees combined to represent about 13,000 eligible city employees—was forced to post a notice reminding its own employees that they couldn't be interrogated about their union sympathies, nor could they be fired for joining another labor union.

The NLRB required HOPE to post the sign for sixty days, after HOPE allegedly fired six employees for their internal union-organizing activities. HOPE also agreed to pay them nearly $36,000 in back wages after they tried to join the FAIR union, according to a settlement agreement approved last year.

By signing the agreement, HOPE did not admit violating federal labor law, according to the 2007 accord. Norm Yen, who is also president of HOPE Local 5-H in Houston, said the union agreed to settle the charges to avoid the cost of going to court.

"We're a union," he said. "We like unions."

He said that while HOPE has recognized FAIR as the bargaining group for its seventeen or so employees, they don't have a contract in place. For more than a year, the two sides haven't found a time to meet, Yen said.

Unions as employers engage in some of the most blatant unfair labor practice activities that have been recorded by the NLRB. Mike Muskat, an attorney with the Houston law firm Muskat, Martinez, and Mahoney, stated in an interview that unions as employers have been found to violate their own employees' rights more often than most people think.

In fact, Mr. Muskat said, when he represented labor organizations as an attorney at a firm in Washington, DC, a good amount of the work he performed was to defend the labor organizations against claims filed by their own employees, many of which included unfair labor practices.

"It's incredible how sympathetic" union management is to the employer's viewpoint, Muskat recalled.

It would seem that charges such as unfair labor practices would be a hassle, embarrassing and expensive to defend for labor unions. You would think that they would conduct themselves with their own employees in a manner that would be above reproach, that they would set a sterling example—set the bar, so to speak, for the companies they criticize or harangue. But strangely enough, unions seem to have a problem observing the laws they so piously preach to employers in the companies they harass. Unions claim that it's disgruntled workers who bring these charges and that the unions are being unfairly hassled. They also claim that some of these charges are a result of intra-union politics when a power struggle between two sides is fully engaged. One side, to embarrass the other side, files charges.

They may be right. All of the above may be quite true. However, when has a union ever given a corporation the same pass they themselves expect to get from the public?

Many companies would like to pass on a message to unions regarding these employee issues: "Welcome to our world!"

So the war on workers continues, with union employees on the frontline against their employer—SEIU.

SEIU claims to be united for workers' dignity, improving the lives of workers and their families, and creating a more just and humane society, according to one of their websites. But improving the lives of their own workers is not on top of their priority list

In March 2009, just before the expiration of their contract on the thirty-first of the month, seventy-five SEIU staffers were laid off.

The SEIU employees then took the next step that a well-trained union member would take in the face of such blatant employer abuse: they picketed their employer, SEIU.

On March 27, 2009, many of the seventy-five employees laid off took to the streets and picketed outside SEIU headquarters in Washington, DC. SEIU had trained their staffers well; they came to their picket line armed with bullhorns and chanting union slogans such as "justice for all, not just some!"

For a union that self-proclaimed itself as the vanguard of the progressive movement, it seems to have a problem with practicing what it preaches. Charges of unfair labor practices and age and race discrimination claims have been filed against the darling of the ultra-left social movement. Quite the hypocrites SEIU officials are, lambasting corporations and companies for greedy behavior when they lay off workers to get lean and mean; yet, they themselves believe they were justified when they felt the need to follow in corporate America's footsteps. What sanctimonious little killjoys.

Of course the layoffs were needed, according to SEIU spokesperson Michelle Ringuette, since SEIU was decentralizing its organizing force and putting the burden of organizing campaigns on their locals. Imagine that...maybe the next time ABC Inc. managers have to lay off people, they can utilize Michelle as a spokesperson for them. Why not offer these organizers the option of a lateral move to a local? Just a thought.

Ms. Ringuette went on to say that this was how SEIU was enacting decisions made at its democratic convention. Members democratically made a decision, and SEIU was responding to that decision. Corporations do the same thing—through decisions made to benefit their members (only they're called stockholders). It is amazing that SEIU does not see the duplicity of its actions. Union officials use the same management tactics they attack corporations for employing, such as terminations without giving an employee proper notice and refusing to meet with their staff prior to the expiration of their own collective-bargaining agreement.

SEIU sees things differently. They feel that the protest is a sign of a "thriving democratic movement." Now *there* is a phrase employers can use the next time SEIU accuses them of being heartless for laying off workers. SEIU further defends its actions by claiming that the laid-off staffers were invited to apply for eighty other positions in the organization, which they were made aware of. Mighty big of them, wouldn't you say?

According to Sam Hananel of the Associated Press, *"Sometimes even unions have union problems."*

This song and dance is very familiar. Following the lead of the International Brotherhood of Teamsters, SEIU moved to decentralize its organizing department. This move would make it harder for organizers to organize a union for themselves. I am sure it was coincidental that both unions seemed to be moving in lockstep with each other. Perhaps the continuous threat of a union-represented workforce forced the unions to take steps that would prevent any collective bargaining agreement from being reached by their own organizers.

It is supremely ironic that SEIU, an organization determined to bring unionization to as many workplaces as possible, fires its own employees, sometimes for trying to form their own union.

In a mockery of the very unionism message they preach to the world, the Service Employees International Union uses tactics no corporate employer would dare try, to prevent the union's employees from organizing. SEIU's former president Andy Stern is fond of saying, "First we will use the power of persuasion, then we will use the persuasion of power." Evidently, that is also applied to its own workers when they run afoul of the powerful union.

SEIU did not limit its anti-union activities to just its International. The infamous ACORN operates in SEIU's Louisiana Locals 880 and 100. SEIU paid ACORN $2.5 million to train the union's employees in the fine art of planning and implementing negative public-relations campaigns against targeted corporations and conservative organizations.

Wade Rathke, ACORN's founder, has a notable history of "union avoidance." In 2003, the National Labor Relations Board found ACORN guilty of illegally busting a unionization drive of its own employees. When Rathke was presented with a petition demanding union recognition, Rathke, his wife, Beth Butler, and his brother Dale Rathke concocted a variety of maneuvers that would make a company union-buster blush, just to avoid having a unionized workforce. Rathke allegedly "tried to red-bait a number of his former organizers." The unionizing drive failed, much to the relief of Rathke and SEIU.

Prewitt Organizing Fund is described as a nonprofit that assists unions and other progressive organizations to create campaigns for organizing and public relations. They deal in public-awareness strategies and recruit organizers to promote and increase union membership. Prewitt Fund spearheaded the organizing drive of online giant

Amazon.com in 2000 at its Fernley, Nevada, location. SEIU also spent another $70,000 on Prewitt as a consultant to the Change to Win Coalition.

In 2006, Prewitt was engaged in a very nasty union-busting campaign of its own. As an SEIU ally, Prewitt received almost $1 million in support from SEIU while facing a battle to bust a union-organizing drive by its own employees. It is alleged that in August 2006, Prewitt fired two staff members for trying to unionize. Prewitt found itself on the receiving end of at least ten complaints of alleged violations of federal labor law. The Prewitt Fund, whose very existence revolves around union organizing in hospitals and corporations, was playing out the ultimate hypocrisy.

> As reported by *SEIU Exposed*:
> *In January 2007, unionized members of SEIU Local 1.on, organized through the Teamsters, went out on strike against SEIU over complaints about low wages. Elsewhere, the union's own employees filed a federal complaint against the union for its behavior as an employer. An announcement from employees said, "SEIU's bullying of its staff continues to be met with resistance" after the union attempted to "force an unfair contract including a demand to waive legally protected rights." It was just the latest evidence of a pattern of SEIU abusing its own staff.*

Labeling SEIU's management as a "well-oiled de facto politburo," former SEIU organizer Kevin Funk exposed his union's hypocrisy, which he argued was "characterized by an often subtle yet convoluted net of deceit, fear-mongering, incompetence, and, in fact, union-busting."

SEIU's record of employee treatment is dismal at best. From Texas to Louisiana and onward to California, SEIU's scorch-and-burn policy toward its staff would be the envy of the most anti-union corporations.

It is the ultimate duplicity that a union decides that it should be able to replace those who work for it on a whim, that a new union administration elected to office should be able to replace the existing staff with its own people. Can you imagine how a corporation would be ostracized if, when it hired a new executive team, that team turned around and fired the current staff in order to bring in the team's own people? Alternatively, as one union member stated, "They don't need a contract. If they do their job they wouldn't have to be worried about being fired." Hmmm, does that same sentiment exist for corporations and their employees? If so, there really is no argument for the continuation of unions representing workers.

The changing face of union organizations is reflected in the move toward the corporate model of unionism in SEIU. Many of the rank and file believe that union work is a form of social and economic activism and that because it is a labor of love or passion for a social cause, those who work for the union should not be represented by a union themselves, that somehow it is unfitting. Many other union employees and staffers would answer such a thought by stating the obvious: an employee is an employee is an employee, no matter who the employer is. Any worker who can be punished, terminated, demoted, transferred, and the like, has the right to be represented by a collective bargaining agreement. As some companies do, some unions treat their staff properly and with respect. But just as unions claim that treatment is not always the case with companies, so it can be said about unions.

Many employees who had worked in the private sector and then went to work for a union have said they were treated worse by the union than their private-sector employer. A union treats its own employees as expendable pawns on a chessboard; how can they possibly claim to be fighting on the side of the working people and to advance those at the bottom of the socioeconomic ladder? They can't, or maybe it would be better stated that they shouldn't.

The fact is that unions, more so than corporations, will hire and fire on a whim or for political expediency. The belief that union staffers who have a collective bargaining agreement would be an intrusion on the important work they were hired to do—really, do these people actually like what they see when they look into a mirror? Why would those who are advocating for the rights of workers, for economic justice for those less fortunate, not be entitled to that which they profess others should have?

If a union does not interfere with the production and profitability of a company, it cannot possibly hinder the work of its own staff members. Unions were created to protect and advance the interest of all workers; that is their cause, their sole reason for existence. Are not their own employees workers also?

Many union staffers have been emboldened to fight harder for their members when represented by a union, claim some SEIU former staffers. Top union officials have written off members who were facing layoffs from an employer. Had the union staffers not had the protection of a union bargaining agreement, they would not have pushed back against the union officials to fight for their members' jobs. And why would union staffers fear for their jobs if they disagree with a higher-up union official? Because, according to most union employees, union officials have a penchant for retaliating against staffers who disagree with them.

Like the rank-and-file Teamsters members, as stated in chapter 1, many union members believe that having union employees protected by a collective bargaining agreement would disrupt the democratic process in the union or hinder attempts to reform a union that members perceive has gone down the wrong path. A unionized staff would make it impossible to fire dishonest, incompetent, or lazy staff, they say. Wow, how crazy is this? Corporations feel the same way. It sounds like corporate employers have much in common with their union counterparts.

Here is my thought on that: unions can fire their employees, too; they just have to follow the same rules and laws that they expect companies to follow. Radical concept, I know, but I was always an out-of-the-box thinker. Yes, it might mean a long process of following the proper procedures, but if a company can manage, so can a union. If a violation is severe enough, then union officials can terminate immediately, since there are laws that would protect that type of termination, and as any union official or member knows, most collective bargaining agreements allow for immediate termination if the violation is severe enough.

Strangely enough, SEIU has chosen a different path. Like Wal-Mart and the other companies they ostracize, SEIU is using every legal loophole to circumvent "just cause" and other protective language in a collective bargaining agreement or to avoid a collective bargaining agreement altogether. SEIU seems determined to be able to terminate or fire staff members who do not fit in with their new ideal of corporate unionism. This ideal changes on the whim of the union official who is in control at the time and follows less-standard operating procedures than those found in corporate America.

One of the tactics SEIU used was to combine a number of locals into a new local. This strategy was put in play to eliminate Local 660 and its obligation to that local's staffers under their collective bargaining agreement. SEIU claimed that since it was a "new" business, it had no obligation to the "former" Local 660 staff workers, including even those covered by the United Union Representatives of Los Angeles (UURLA) contract. When businesses do this, unions are rightly outraged. This activity would bring a tear to even the most practiced union-buster's eye.

There is a movement among some of the major labor unions to emulate SEIU's organizational model, as stated earlier in discussing the Teamsters' actions with their own employees. Union members get caught in the middle of this war on union employees and often find that they suffer by receiving poor representation. The rank and file find themselves asking whether their own representatives or union office workers deserve to be represented.

When a union moves to corporatization, does it not lose the soul of what it was founded on? When an organization that was created to represent the worker turns to only representing its own self-interest, what is the point of its existence? When a union moves toward a corporate model of unionism, the members lose because they lose their voice and any meaningful decision-making power, the staff loses because they unfairly lose their jobs, and the members lose again because the staffers targeted for termination are often those most committed to empowering the members—not empowering their politically motivated bosses.

The meaning of corporate unionism is that unions begin to look more like corporations than unions. The hierarchy resembles less a democratically controlled representative model and more a top-down authority. Elected union presidents resemble their corporate CEO counterparts. With all the power that comes from an executive board that has thrown in with the elected president, rules change to make it harder to remove an incumbent from power. This automatically erodes the democratic process and silences the voices of those who work for the union, as well as those who believe they are represented by it. With no control over the decision-making process, those who would otherwise disagree with officials who enact mandates become accessories to those centralizing the union's power for fear of retaliation should they speak out.

The work that front-line union workers did, believing they would be empowering workers by building stewards councils and other structures, is being undermined by SEIU's turn toward corporate unionism.

To repeat the earlier statement by Sam Hananel of the Associated Press, sometimes even unions have union problems.

If Texas and California SEIU workers thought they were being abused, they should reach out to their brothers and sisters who worked for other unions. In other words, SEIU and the Teamsters are not isolated in the actions against their own employees.

Chapter 3
UAW Downsizes Its Own Company

While the United Auto Workers cried, stamped their feet, and predicted doom for the United States if the federal government didn't step in to bail out GM and Chrysler, they seemed to have no problem downsizing their own company a decade before the big auto bailout. Of course, laying off members interferes directly with their revenue, whereas treating their own employees as expendable just increases the payday in the pockets of the executive board.

In this case, the UAW bought a radio station back in 1996. Why the United Auto Workers would buy a radio station lines right up there with why they would believe an upscale golf resort would be a boon to trade training—they bought one of those, too. Like any corporation, the United Auto Workers must have felt the need to diversify. Moreover, in the tradition of the United Auto Workers, they managed to drive their own United Broadcasting Network radio station into bankruptcy.

This whole ordeal did not capture the nation's attention like the financial perils of the big three auto companies at the end of 2007, but the people involved found that having the UAW as an employer was not an exercise in workers' rights. After terminating approximately forty-three employees, the UAW found itself on the receiving end of a lawsuit in which their former employees accused the union of terminating them without cause and purposely navigating the radio station into the abyss of bankruptcy.

The drama unfolded in a series of court actions that took place in both Florida and Michigan. The circumstances reeked of hypocrisy. As the UAW fired its own employees at the United Broadcasting Network, it was demanding job security as it entered into contract negotiations with the big three, Chrysler Daimler, Ford, and General Motors. A review of several thousand pages of correspondence, court filings, testimony transcripts, and interviews with former UBN employees and management raises questions about how the UAW conducts business and treats its workers.

To get a clear picture of why the UAW found itself the target of its former employees' wrath, you have to get a glimpse of the history of UAW becoming a radio station owner.

The names of the people involved in this fiasco might ring a bell to those who follow politics and/or talk radio. United Broadcasting started its life as the People's Network, a nonprofit organization owned by radio talk-show star Chuck Harder. There was a point in his career when Chuck Harder was second only to Rush Limbaugh in the size of his audience. Chuck's troubles started when he ran afoul of the IRS. Harder, who was considered one of the most influential talk-show hosts in the United States, was facing a battle with the IRS after an audit in which the IRS claimed that Harder owed over $1 million in back taxes. Unless he could pay the back taxes and fines, Harder would be forced off the air.

Harder often talked to his audience about his IRS problems and that they were the result of his crippling commentary of the Clinton administration. Bill Clinton was president at the time. In 1994, Chuck Harder turned to Pat Choate for help with his IRS problem. Pat Choate was an author and economist, as well as a radio commentator himself. Harder believed that Choate's network of people in Washington would be able to get him out of his bind with the IRS. For those of you who think that Pat Choate's name is tickling some long-forgotten memory, you would be right: Pat Choate was also the running mate of Ross Perot.

Harder and Choate saw eye to eye in several areas, one of them being the promotion of "made in the USA" consumerism. While Harder may have had more on-air talent than Choate did, it was Choate who had the talent when it came to moneymaking ideas. In fact, he was called the "entrepreneur of ideas." When Choate looked at the People's Network, he saw the start of a beautiful thing. In Choate's mind, if the network was converted into a for-profit network and seeded with top on-air talent who, regardless of political belief, would all work toward promoting "made in the USA," it would be a success. Choate felt that the People's Network Harder had created could become a leader in the talk-radio universe, especially after the Communications Act of 1996.

An investment of $10 million was what Choate set as the capital needed to turn the People's Network into what he believed it could become. Enter the UAW. Like Choate and Harder, the UAW had a commitment to buying USA-made products. Their membership had been preaching that very mantra since Toyota started knocking on their door in the 1970s. Even better, because of that very membership, the UAW had the cash!

The UAW launched the now-renamed network, United Broadcasting Network (UBN), with $5 million. Pat Choate led an experienced management team to run the day-to-day operations of the radio station. In April 1996, the Florida-based United Broadcasting Network was officially owned by a partnership that included the UAW. Part of the agreement between the partners and UAW was that the union would have veto power on the board of directors. Faster than the UAW can say "bailout," the union took control of even the most mundane operating decisions of the network.

From the moment the ink was dry, UAW representatives complained about the way the network was being run. In a ruthless move that Leona Helmsley would envy, the UAW started to purge the network of its existing staff. More than 50 percent of the people employed by the network were terminated in the following two years. The next series of maneuvers by the UAW left it as the sole owner of UBN by 1997. Also in 1997, UBN filed for bankruptcy in Michigan, even though the network had been incorporated in Delaware.

What had once been a two-hundred-station radio network was now down to only sixty. Looks like the UAW had the same effect on the broadcasting business as it had on the auto industry. But what subsequent lawsuits revealed was a diabolical plan that treated the employees of the now-defunct network as nothing more than pawns.

The beginning of the end started with Chuck Harder and Pat Choate—the former apparently offending the Clintons with his brash opinion about their job performance, and the latter accepting the number two spot on Ross Perot's Reform Party ticket. While some say it was President Bush who had it in for Chuck Harder, even Harder admitted that it was actually the Clintons who really had it in for him.

The UAW, a union, was now a managing partner of UBN. That did not deter Harder from voicing his opinion on Clinton's job performance as president—an opinion that was often critical and caustic. Harder was against NAFTA (North American Free Trade Act) and GATT (General Agreement on Tariffs and Trade), among other things that the Clinton administration was hawking to the public. These are areas where the UAW should have been firmly behind Harder.

But never let it be said that workers' rights ever stood between a union and its political party. With Clinton running for reelection, the UAW was not pleased with the direction Harder was taking and made it clear that his disparagement of President Clinton had to end—and end now. It was said that Hillary Clinton had made a comment to one of the UAW officials regarding the fact that they invested in a network that employed a talk-show host who continually condemned President Clinton's policies, when they would have been better off investing in her brother's radio program. Harder was like any talk-show host and refused to change his diatribe against the incumbent president.

The purchase of the network still had not closed, and Harder believed that the UAW would not live up to its end of the bargain with him, which he desperately needed. With the advantage firmly in the UAW's hands, Harder was "leaned on" until he agreed to a leave of absence until after the elections were over. Along with his vacating the show for those two months, he was forced into giving up his 25 percent partnership in the network.

As if Harder did not cause the UAW enough grief with the Clinton White House, the union now had to contend with a partner who was running against the incumbent president. Steve Yokich, the international president for the UAW at the time, was reported to have screamed, "The UAW is now putting money into a radio network whose leader is running hard against the Clinton White House! How the hell do I explain this to Harold Ickes (manager of the Clinton reelection campaign)?"

At the time, the UAW president had every reason to be "freaking." Ross Perot had asked Choate to be his running mate, and Choate had accepted. The only hang-up was that Choate had to wait for the new deal with Harder to be settled. Choate, however, informed the UAW that he intended to be the vice president on the Perot Reform Party ticket. Steve Yokich, must have been flirting with cardiac arrest when he heard the news of Choate's plans. Polls showed that Perot was a definite threat in the battleground states, such as Michigan. Just as the Republicans believed that Ross Perot could cost Bob Dole the election, the Democrats were afraid Perot would pull enough support and cost Clinton the election. It's tough being the third-party candidate; everyone fears you, and hence everyone hates you. Choate's exit from the network commenced; he stepped down as chairman of the board and also complied with the demand that he not show up at the network for the remainder of the campaign season.

Now there is nothing like cleaning out upper management to make employees start to worry about their own fate. According to all reports, an employee by the name of David Hand began to think about job security, which led to him believe that maybe the workers at UBN needed to be represented by a union in a collective bargaining agreement between UBN and UAW. It made perfect sense to Hand and the other employees he had talked to. Unfortunately, David Hand was never a union organizer—he was a producer. Had he been an organizer at any time in his life, he would have known not to discuss his plans to organize with his employer. After meetings with his coworkers, Hand presented his employer, the UAW, with a list of concerns. David Hand was terminated soon after he discussed with his UAW bosses his plans to unionize.

Unlike corporations, unions are vindictive, and when Hand filed for his unemployment benefits, UBN countered his right to those benefits based on what they stated was his failure to work up to unspecified standards, even though his evaluations up until the point he was fired were stellar. In front of the Florida Department of Labor and Employment Security's (DLES) Division of Unemployment Compensation, Hand countered with the defense that he was not fired for poor performance, but for trying to organize a union among his coworkers. In 1997, after looking at all the arguments and documents provided by both sides, DLES ruled in favor of David Hand and found the United Auto Workers union guilty of terminating one of its employees because of his organizing activities.

After Choate and Hand, the UAW's management ax men started to lop off heads; terminations became as rapid as the layoffs at GM in the beginning of 2008. Where was the government to save these employees' jobs...anyone...anyone? Employees described the UAW henchmen's activities as the "alphabet firings." The name was coined because employees felt that UAW took an alphabetical list of employees and, starting at the top, began firing everyone on it. Out of a staff of seventy, forty-three did not survive the purge.

To add insult to injury, the UAW did not even mail out the terminated employees' final paychecks or owed vacation pay. I wonder if Ford could get away with that. The list of those who were denied their severance and accrued vacation pay included two African Americans (is this racism by the UAW?) and a handicapped employee who worked from home (which smacks of discrimination).

Let the court battles begin. Employees sued the United Auto Workers for the forfeiture of their positions with the now-bankrupt radio network. They claimed that the network was profitable until the UAW, with malicious intent, manipulated the company into bankruptcy in a coup for control. According to statements made by employees at the UBN order-processing center, UBN was making money during 1996. Employees claimed they were receiving more orders for made-in-the-USA products than ever before. In addition to the surge in sales, the daily programming distribution was up.

The United Auto Workers responded by filing a separate lawsuit against its partners at UBN, claiming excessive spending on things such as airline tickets. Seriously? Has the UAW looked at their own LM-2s (federal annual financial reports) and seen how much they themselves spent on airline tickets for so-called "union business"?

Jumping onto the lawsuit carousel, the UAW's partners in the network have themselves filed suit against the UAW for breach of contract. Their claims are far more interesting. In their suit, the partners claimed that the UAW purposely drove down the worth of United Broadcasting Network. What would the UAW gain by driving down the value of a business it was a partner in? According to the partners, it was so the UAW could assume sole control of the network and maintain only the propaganda side of the station to promote the UAW political agenda.

UAW International President Steven Yokich, UAW Public Relations Director Frank Joyce, and UAW Chief Counsel Dan Sherrick claimed "executive privilege" of sorts by trying to prevent testimony, which included videotape of UAW officials taken in a case the UAW had brought to court earlier. The case made its way to court in 2001. The UAW's attorneys put forth a case that was described by all spectators as brilliant. The Michigan jury found in favor of the UAW.

In an article written by Robert Mundy and published by *Insight* in August 1999, former UBN employee Rebecca Fox explained her treatment as a worker by the UAW:

> So in May 1996, when the new owners at UBN, one of the few non-state employers in this rural town, promised medical coverage for employees such as Fox and her daughter, her coworkers were surprised that she voiced skepticism about the guarantees being made.
>
> But the new owners of UBN were different, her coworkers assured her. After all, backing this venture was a huge organization (UAW) which proclaims, "We are the only institution that stands up for working men and women."

Chapter 4
Union Calls Out Another Union for Unfair Labor Practices

You've got to love a union that has the moxie to practice employer strategy at the negotiating table. You have to really admire the audacity of a union that practices bad faith regarding a contract negotiation and finds nothing wrong with that. The best part of this story, though, is that it was the union's in-house attorneys who were on the receiving end.

It seems that the Milwaukee-based Office and Professional Employees International Union (OPEIU) Local 9 had to file unfair labor-practice charges against fellow union, Local 150 of the International Union of Operating Engineers (IUOE), headquartered in Countryside, Illinois.

According to the National Labor Relations Board charges OPEIU filed against the IUOE, the employers unilaterally changed the work schedules of the attorneys who worked for them without first consulting with OPEIU. In addition, they accused the Operating Engineers with failing to bargain in good faith over concerns of the attorneys' employment.

The lawyers had become a collective bargaining unit in the summer of 2011, and as of this writing (January 2012), were still negotiating in an attempt to reach an agreement for the first contract.

OPEIU Local 9 has approximately 750 active members in Wisconsin, Illinois, Indiana, and Iowa. Most of them perform clerical work for other labor groups.

In an article for the *Chicago Union News*, Dawn Martin, a business manager for OPEIU Local 9, told Katie Drew:

> *"It's difficult for unions to serve in the role as employer.*
>
> *"It can be very challenging, I think, because they start to become the very people that they will be across the table from," Martin continued. "Sometimes you need to remind them that while they are the employer, they are still the union, and their employees need to be treated the same way their members need to be treated."*
>
> *Martin said she is awaiting a response from Local 150 regarding the charges her union filed against the other.*
>
> *"Hopefully we can get this out in the negotiating process," Martin said. "I think there is a desire on the part of all parties to get this resolved without going to a hearing."*

Operating Engineers Local 150 represents both active and retired engineers in Illinois, Indiana, and Iowa. It boasts a membership of over twenty thousand workers.

Ed Maher, a representative for Local 150, told the *Chicago Union News* that *"negotiating the first agreement is a very complex process but both sides are committed to working toward a mutually beneficial agreement."*

The two sides had scheduled bargaining sessions for January 30 and 31, 2012. The NLRB had set a hearing for February 23.

Chapter 5

A Company that Gets a Union Deserves a Union

No wonder nonunion UFCW reps want a union at their jobs:

A union filed a petition (5-RC-16629) with the National Labor Relations Board office in Baltimore, Maryland, asking the NLRB to conduct a secret-ballot election. The employer in this case happens to be the United Food and Commercial Workers (UFCW) Local 400, based in Landover, Maryland. The petitioning union is the Federation of Agents and International Representatives (FAIR).

Two weeks before Valentine's Day in 2011, a group of UFCW union representatives filed a petition for union recognition. I guess they weren't feeling the love from their employer, UFCW Local 400. With the filing of the petition comes the secret ballot election that would be scheduled by the NLRB.

UFCW is another union that supported the Employee Free Choice Act for corporations, but failed to practice what they proposed inside the walls of its own business. Instead of recognizing the bargaining unit, as they encourage corporations to do, UFCW Local 400 came out swinging in a manner that would make so-called union-busters blush.

The following was posted on several websites, including Redstate and LUR. It is reprinted here as it appeared:

> *Sandi Stokes on February 10, 2011 at 8:24 pm*
> *Local 400 is an excellent place of employment and should be viewed as a model of how a workplace should operate and conduct business. There is no hypocrisy what so ever. The entire issue is really about employees (Representatives) who are completely clueless, unappreciative, and incompetent. They seek unwarranted promotions and other*

types of rewards and contribute very little. Local 400 reorganized to ensure that our cause is really about the "union members." These Representatives have been skating and underperforming which is no longer tolerated. Now that they are being held to very high performance standards, they run to FAIR for shelter. What you have reported on your website is completely untrue and is being fueled by those few narcissistic individuals whose low work ethic would not be permitted at any other workplace. Local 400 has given these Representatives a chance to step up to the cause, our members. The outcome of the election will not change the expectation of these Representatives to not only meet but exceed high performance standards; Local 400 is no different than any other employer.

Wow, can you say "hypocrite!"? These are the same people who would initiate a PR nightmare for any grocery chain that responded that way to an attempt by its employees to unionize. Can they really be that blind to the hypocrisy and double standard they wish to promote? Their defense rests solely on the quality of service to the members. So if a grocery chain were to take this post, replace the words *representative* with *employee* and *members* with *customers*, would that fly for Ms. Stokes and the UFCW if they were attempting to organize that store?

You might think that Sandi Stokes must be just a member or someone without authority, because certainly the UFCW officers would not make such a calamitous mistake—and in writing, no less. Well, let's all meet Sandi Stokes.

According to federal law, the Landrum Griffith Act, every union must file what is called an LM-2. The LM-2 is a labor management report that lists all of the union's officers and staff, as well as what they earn and any other compensation or reimbursement handed out. It also reports the number of members and all financial aspects of the union. These records are public information, and any person can access them through the US Department of Labor website.

In 2009, the UFCW Local 400 listed Sandi Stokes as the comptroller for the local. As comptroller, her earnings were listed at $103,000 per year. Gee, I wonder what the grocery-store clerks who pay for her wage make? The comptroller is equivalent to the office manager; some locals have both, while others, because of their size, may have only one person who does double duty. But whatever the composition of the local, one thing is for sure: her position in any private company would put her squarely in a management capacity.

The UFCW as an employer does not seem to hold its workers in high esteem. May I recommend labor relation classes? Perhaps if the management of Local 400 communicated better and allowed their workers a voice in the workplace, this would not happen. Maybe the workers felt they lacked respected from their superiors and saw a contractual bargaining agreement as the only way to achieve a respectful environment. Maybe they were tired of being hauled into their boss's office and told how pathetic they were, without a steward there to represent them. Whatever the case, if I worked for that woman, I might be looking at a union, too!

Yes, sometimes union representatives actually have unions represent them against their exploitive employers—the unions.

Unions have never found a corporate practice that they cannot co-opt and even improve on. That is true also in the area of "union busting." While companies stumble along, hiring legal counsel and consultants to carry out a campaign that they themselves are amateurs players in, the unions are ruthless and wicked in their persecution of staff who choose to try to organize a union. They are often guilty of violating the very laws they accuse employers of violating. Their disregard for the rights of their own employees is in direct contrast to the sermons they preach on workers' rights to a public audience. In fact, going by the measure they use when criticizing conservatives, they really should be Republicans. It is actually a hobby for union representatives to engage in union-busting activity, and the cleverer they are, the more apt they are to brag about their successes.

While UFCW Local 400 was demeaning and badmouthing its employees for wanting to unionize, the UFT (United Federation of Teachers) skipped the standard spitefulness and character assassination, and went straight to termination for a longtime staffer who was attempting to organize UFT employees.

Not wanting to be left out of the "in crowd," the UAW imposed its own austerity measures on its staffers while crying foul when the same was attempted for the auto industry's union members several years ago. And of course, as previously mentioned, there is the infamous Teamsters union—Jimmy Hoffa Jr. playing hardball with union staff when they threatened a walkout in 2009 over a proposed substandard contract offered by the Teamsters International.

The ultimate in union busting, of course, is SEIU, which has taken it to an art form that would be the envy of those in the corporate world if only they could violate the law as cleverly as the union bosses do.

Since these unions seemed to be successful in not only union busting, but also having an absolute party doing it, Amalgamated Transit Union (ATU) came to the party and surpassed all expectations when it came to intimidating its own union-forming staff. ATU represents workers who operate in the transportation industry, with the exception of trucking, air travel, trains, and anything requiring water. What's left? Well, honestly, not much. Every now and then it attempts to organize the dealers at the Wynn Casino for fun. I mean I can see the connection—transportation and dealers: those are just two industries that naturally go together.

ATU is the union that seldom gets any respect. It is the Rodney Dangerfield of the union world. So it, in turn, decided, hey, let's do something big, like you know, unashamedly deprive our own employees of the right to organize, which is protected under the National Labor Relations Act. Hey, that should get us some respect from the real unions. So proceeding with this idea, which was obviously formulated by one of its brighter minds, ATU outright fired an employee for signing a union representation card. Now, although other unions do this all the time, there is a reason why ATU gets no respect from unions wearing big-boy pants: they got caught.

David Highnote, assistant director of communications at ATU, was organizing to form an in-house union to represent the professional staff as a bargaining unit of the Washington-Baltimore Newspaper Guild. The newly elected president of the ATU, Larry Hanley, was not thrilled with this out-of-the-box thinking on the part of his staffer. After all, like any corporation, unions like team players, and forming a union while being employed by a union...well, Hanley felt that was just plain un-team-player-like. So in an attempt to establish his tough-guy image, being that he was new and all at the job, Hanley sent his henchmen (Hanley's Henchmen—should be a band) to talk some sense into this obviously misguided man. After all, who needs a union?

Unfortunately for Hanley and the henchmen, Highnote reported being told, "I only want to say this once. Larry (Hanley) is sensitive to all of the things going on in and outside of the office. If we find out that you are discussing workplace conditions with coworkers or anyone else, then one strike and you're out." This employee mentoring took place two weeks after Mr. Highnote had signed his union authorization card. Undeterred, Highnote practiced what his union preached to nonunion dealers at the Wynn Casino—"Don't let them scare you into backing down"—and he continued to push union solidarity among his coworkers.

Hanley was newly elected under a cloud of alleged election fraud. The corruption and illegal allegations were convincing enough that the US Department of Labor launched its own investigation into Hanley's election practices. The accusations surrounding Hanley involved threats and intimidation of supporters of candidates running against him.

When David Highnote was terminated, it was done under the pretext of a structural reorganization by the newly elected administration. The problem with that explanation was that after they fired Highnote, they immediately hired someone else to fill the very same position. Under the NLRA, that dog just won't hunt.

David Highnote proceeded to file "Unfair Labor Practice Complaint with National Labor Relations Board Charges Amalgamated Transit Union (ATU) International President and AFL-CIO Executive Council Member Larry Hanley with Discriminatory Discharge of Union Employee for Organizing In-House Union for ATU Professional Staff, and Other Protected Activities, in Violation of the National Labor Relations Act" on April 12, 2011.

Having been accused of being a union-buster myself, at this point I can only roll around on the floor, laughing hysterically.

Book Two
Just Walk Away

Chapter 6
No Happy Union Ending

"To a right-winger, unions are awful. Why do right-wingers hate unions? Because collective bargaining is the power that a worker has against the corporation. Right-wingers hate that."
—Janeane Garofalo, *Majority Report*, June 3, 2010

If what the esteemed and intellectually challenged Ms. Garofalo said in the above quote is correct, then the American worker is surely without a champion. Consider the case of the Teamsters' abandonment of one newly organized group of workers.

The following Joint Council 25 announcement was posted on the Chicago Teamsters website:

> *Precast Workers Vote to Join Teamsters*
> *Amid Anti-Union Assault, Aurora Workers Organize With Teamsters Local 673*
> *Approximately 80 workers with ATMI Precast in Aurora have voted in favor of Teamster representation after enduring a lengthy anti-union campaign.*
> *In an effort to prevent the Teamster victory, ATMI management screened anti-union videos, conducted captive-audience meetings and hired several union-busting consultants, while supervisors regularly wore anti-union pins. Teamsters Local 673 is now preparing to negotiate the first contract for workers, who cited a lack of respect, workplace safety and affordable health care options in their decision to organize.*
> *"The workers were able to overcome the company's persistent anti-union push through a combination of efforts by the local union and the organizing department of Teamsters Joint Council 25," said Roger Kohler, Secretary-Treasurer of Local 673.*
> *The employees—98 percent of whom are Hispanic—represent a broad range of laborers at one of the largest precast manufacturers in*

the tri-state area, including blasters, yard patchers, forklift operators, steel shaft welders and woodshop employees.

"The workers are in need of a fair wage for their labor and the right to a grievance procedure to address working conditions," Kohler said. "The workers know the Teamsters will secure a better standard of living for them and their families at the bargaining table."

Teamsters Local 673 is an affiliate of Teamsters Joint Council 25, which represents more than 100,000 hardworking men and women throughout Illinois and Indiana.

But a happy union ending was not destined for the workers at ATMI Precast. As posted on Teamster.net: *"You voted the companies proposal down for the third time, you're on your own" said Javier, a representative of the Teamsters' Union, to the ATMI before they were locked out.*

ATMI Precast, an Aurora, Illinois , company creates precast concrete products. Contract negotiations between the company and Teamsters Local 673 had been ongoing since March 2010. The Teamsters had won the election to represent ATMI's production and maintenance employees. According to news reports, the company had made significant compromises, and in its last offer to the union members, offered a wage increase. However, the new Teamsters members were not pleased with the last offer and on November 5 voted it down. They soon found themselves on the other end of a lockout.

Normally, when a union turns down a last, best, and final offer from a company, it is the union that strikes, but ATMI turned the tables on the union and its own employees. It hired temporary workers to do the work its permanent employees would not be doing.

The previous year, ATMI had instituted a 20 percent wage cut for hourly workers, which was the catalyst for the workers to petition for a union election. The Teamsters came out victorious, but at the end of a lengthy negotiation process, could only deliver a 5 percent wage increase over five years to their new members.

It appears that the organizer, true to form, promised a union dream to workers, but the truth became more of a union nightmare for the embattled workers, who believed what they had been promised.

The Teamsters appeared to have turned their backs on the hapless workers of ATMI. Union organizers often encourage workers to join the union, sign a card, not worry about putting everything on the line, the union will protect them. Yet when the workers of ATMI were locked out, where were the Teamsters then? Missing in action. You can't help but feel for those people locked out right before Christmas.

How did it get to that point, and why would the union, an organization by the workers and for the workers, turn its back on these employees? Well, any organizer will tell you as a prospective member that this is your union, but maybe not so much for ATMI Precast workers. For the Teamsters, maybe standing up for the working man means standing up for something when no one will argue with what you're standing for, or maybe it means only when it's an easy win. Whatever the case, Teamsters Local 673 decided that standing by the ATMI employees just wasn't worth the trouble and abandoned them for easier pickings somewhere else.

To add insult to injury, Teamsters truck drivers were still delivering to the company that locked out their own newly organized members. How is that for a smack in the head? The workers had no support from Local 673, which failed to negotiate a first contract for the very people who put their livelihoods in its hands. The lockout affected 150 workers in the production and maintenance departments. While approximately 80 workers walked a line outside the company, the union was conspicuously absent.

The employees watched as temporary workers took their place inside the plant and their paychecks.

The employees, mostly immigrants from Mexico and South America, claimed that they just wanted their 20 percent wage-cut back, as the company had promised. While they said they understood the economy was poor, there were times when the company was making a profit and instead of giving the workers a share of the profits, it bought new equipment. No raises, just more-expensive insurance. The Teamsters promised that with a union, that would not have happened. With a union, organizers claimed, employees who had been working there for twenty years would not still be making close to minimum wage. With a union, they would have a voice in their workplace; they would have respect.

The company did not want issues with the union, and it claimed a desire to find a solution to the issues as soon as possible. However, that didn't stop ATMI from locking out its employees on November 14 and assuring its customers that they would not suffer a disruption in service. The employees refused to bend on their demands and insisted they just wanted what was fair to them. The men said they planned on picketing in front of the company until they got their jobs back.

> Posted on a Teamsters chat board:
> *Dec. 1 11:45 115 N. State St. Aurora (Immigrant Hope Center, Centro Dristo Rey)*
> *12 noon until 1—march to ATMI Precast 960 Ridgeway Ave.#2 Aurora*
> *Show support for locked-out workers*
> *Dec 2 Monthly rally for jobs 1725 N. Farnsworth, Aurora. Office of*
> *Minute Men of Illinois, a Temporary Work Agency which is supplying untrained "replacement workers" to ATMI.*
> *Posted December 01 2011—03:10 AM*
> *AURORA—March to support ATMI workers, 12 p.m. Plaza Mexico, 700 E. New York Ave. 1 p.m. arrive at ATMI precast, 960 Ridgeway Ave.*

As you would expect, the Teamsters came out swinging in their passionate fight for the working man. Wait minute—that's not what happened? No, instead Teamsters Local 673 on or around November 28 informed ATMI Precast that it no longer represented the employees of the company.

ATMI chief operating officer Paul Carr broke the news in a press release issued Monday that the company had ended the lockout because Teamsters Local 673 officials announced they would not represent ATMI workers.

"ATMI notified all previously locked out employees that they were free to return to work on November 30, 2011. On November 30,

2011, a majority of those employees returned to work," Carr wrote. "On Dec. 1, 2011, I met with the employees and ATMI instituted the wage terms of its last offer to the union—a wage increase and a year-end bonus, for all plant employees subject to the lockout."

The workers at ATMI Precast then took the advice that Hoffa gave to the International Brotherhood of Teamsters' own organizers: they found another union, Laborers Local 681.

On September 1, 2010, the website LaborUnionReport.com posted the following announcement:

Teamsters Union Wins 2010 Most Decertified Union Award
The International Brotherhood of Teamsters is the winner of Union Free America's 5th Annual "Most Decertified Union Award." This honor is awarded to the labor union that lost the most decertification elections during the preceding 12 months. A decertification vote is when the members of a union have had enough of paying for nothing and circulate a petition to trigger a vote to rid themselves of this encumbrance.

The judging was based on an analysis of the reports of election results on the National Labor Relations Board's web site for the period August 2009 through July 2010. During that time the NLRB conducted 251 decertification elections. Employees seeking to rid themselves of a union won 157 or 63 percent of them.

The Teamsters union won the "Most Decertified Union Award" by being decertified 48 times during that period. The Teamsters were involved in a total of 64 decertification elections of which they lost 75 percent.

Chapter 7
Backroom Deals by US Service Unions Strip Workers of Rights

"SEIU/UNITE HERE assume role of labor contractors," says the headline.

Those of us who have been following the infamous SEIU would not be surprised to find that its officials engaged in backroom deals to the detriment of the union's members. It became more than speculation when in May 2008 it was revealed that SEIU and its cohort in dastardly deeds, Unite Here, had entered into a hush-hush deal with Sodexho and Compass Group USA, two of their largest employers under contract.

Andy Stern's purple wave of organizers had a secret to their organizing juggernaut, which had helped build the union's membership to an inspiring 1.8 million members.

The deal seemed to benefit the unions' coffers by giving up their members' rights. The unions agreed to give up the rights to strike, to criticize management, and to establish informational picket lines at different employer sites. In addition to such a generous giveaway, SEIU, just to sweeten an already sweet deal, in offering it to the employers, included the surrender of rights to conduct any organizing drives at any location that the management did not approve of first.

Sodexho and the Compass Group USA provide contract workers to clients such as hospitals and universities. The agreement with the unions went on to specify the number of workers at each company and the actual worksites that could be organized. Aramark, a third employer, was in the process at the time of renegotiating its contract. Good Lord, I would line up, too! What an amazing deal: the companies get to control the union, the unions get more money through dues of newly organized sites picked by the employers, and the employees...unions clandestinely working with companies to deny their employees' rights to concerted activity. There should be a law against that. Wait a minute...

These sweetheart deals netted SEIU and Unite Here 15,000 new members. The story originally was uncovered by the *Wall Street Journal*. Out of the 300,000 people employed by the three companies involved, only about 5 percent of the workers would be under a collective bargaining agreement. Hell of a deal if you can get it.

The *Wall Street Journal* said it based its report on internal union documents. A summary report notes: "Local unions are not free to engage in organizing activities at any Compass or Sodexho locations unless the sites have been designated." It advises that all information regarding union-employer collusion be kept secret from workers, saying it is important "that we honor the confidentiality and not publicly disclose the existence of these agreements."

In 2005, SEIU, with Andy Stern at the helm, led a revolution against the AFL-CIO. It must have been a bitter pill to swallow by then AFL-CIO leader John Sweeney, who mentored Stern when he was an up-and-comer in the union world. Following the lead of SEIU, six unions—SEIU, Unite Here, United Food and Commercial Workers, Carpenters, Laborers, and Teamsters—formed the Change to Win Coalition. They claimed that the AFL-CIO was negligent in its organizing efforts, and the new coalition promised a vigorous new approach to organizing. Rumors persist that this was what the unions fed to the members and the public; according to those inside, there were other reasons for the breakaway.

One of the issues pushed by the Change to Win Coalition was the mandating of smaller unions to merge with the larger ones—kind of a legal way of appropriating other organizations' assets. The other issue, according to those close to the matter, was to eventually pressure Sweeney into resigning so that Richard Trumka could step into the leadership role. In 2009 Sweeney finally resigned—the loss of $30 million per year in membership dues from the breakaway unions proved to be too much—and Trumka took up the reins of the organization. Then those prodigal unions making up the Change to Win coalition returned to the AFL-CIO fold.

The drama unfolded in front of a very disinterested public. Those who were interested proclaimed that the unions were fracturing, weakening, and had turned on their own. Nothing could be further from the truth; in fact they were reinventing themselves. These moves and countermoves had little, if anything, to do with protecting or improving conditions, but involved colluding with shady employers to foist union membership on low-paid workers who were deprived of the right to vote on union membership and in some cases didn't even realize they were joining a union.

While all this drama was playing out like a poorly written plot in an off-Broadway play, Andy Stern had his own rebellion to contend with from an opponent within the SEIU. Sal Rosselli, who led the largest SEIU local in California, criticized Stern for creating an image of SEIU as a collaborator with employers to control the labor force.

Rosselli came into conflict with Stern over renewal of a secret agreement that SEIU set up in 2003 with a group of California nursing-home chains. The arrangement traded a noninterference promise for a pledge by the SEIU to back higher state funding for nursing-home operations and an employer-sponsored "tort reform" law that would limit patients' rights to sue for negligence. The secret agreement also included SEIU's resistance to any legislation that would create staffing levels that the employer did not agree with. Rosselli's public denunciation of Stern put him in jeopardy. Stern is an unforgiving man, and in January 2009, he placed Rosselli's local into trusteeship, effectively kicking the man out of his own local.

Before all of this SEIU political intrigue, the *San Francisco Weekly* in 2007 had reported that the SEIU agreement with the various nursing-home operators had in fact solidified the employers' authoritarianism over its employees. The *Weekly* based its article on internal union documents. Perhaps the most horrifying part of this corruption was the existence of "template agreements." According to the *Weekly*, these restricted nursing-home staff from reporting health and safety violations to regulators, public officials, or the news media, except where obliged to by law because of their despicable nature.

Doesn't warm the heart to know that these unions that cry foul and scream about respect and dignity are on the front lines of taking that away from not only the employees of a nursing home, but also the residents.

To complete the abject loss of any voice in their workplace, SEIU approved conditions that would take away a worker's voice regarding hours, vacations, pay, layoffs, staffing levels, or anything else work related. The article continued:

> *"The employers may outsource work performed by union members, and speed up, reassign, or eliminate jobs at will. The employer may eliminate vacations, or any time off, as the employer sees fit.*
>
> *"The agreement also guarantees that workers' wages will not put an employer at an 'economic disadvantage,' either through employee pay, benefits, or through staff-per-patient ratios."*

I bet those employees felt much better knowing that they had a union—SEIU no less—to protect them from an evil employer. Had those employees been nonunion, they would have had a voice in their workplace.

In other words, under the terms imposed by the SEIU, workers had far fewer rights than if they had no union. Tell me, when an organization that was created to protect workers from employers not only fails in that promise, but engages in activity to further oppress the workers, why should it not be dismantled?

The SEIU thought it had stumbled onto such a great plan that it used the same agreements in Washington state and New Jersey.

Those rascally unions completely abandoned any pretense of representation and "bottom-up" organizations. The stellar example set by SEIU is being followed by other defenders of the blue-collar sector. UFCW and Teamsters think these tactics are just a dandy idea and have started implementing them within their own contracts. Say it ain't so, fellas. With unions like these, who needs evil corporations?

However, let us not just beat up on those fine examples of defenders of the abused masses. After all, the UAW would feel left out if we didn't mention its talent at dumping its members into a substandard agreement. The United Auto Workers negotiated a furtive honey-coated agreement promising an inferior contract in exchange for employer noninterference at a Freightliner plant in Cleveland, North Carolina, in 2003. Five UAW local officials lost their jobs when they launched a strike against the concessions that had been put in the sellout agreement.

It is symbolic of the dilapidated state of the trade unions that some of the harshest criticisms of these substandard agreements—these oppressive deals that further step on the necks of the blue-collar worker and amount to little more than collusion—are announced on the pages of the *Wall Street Journal*.

If these unions want to look at a union-buster, they have only to go as far as the nearest mirror. At least those who engage in the role of labor-relations consultants are honest about what they do for a living.

Chapter 8
Sellout in the Great White Hey

The United States is not alone in the questionable way unions conduct themselves to the detriment of their members. It seems that our neighbors to the north also get to taste corporate unionism at the hands of their union officials.

Dirty deeds done dirt cheap.

Kevin Corporon would tell service industry workers that they were entitled to an honest and decent union. In 1984 Kevin was at the top of his game and had led an enthusiastic organizing drive of the Swiss Chalet Restaurant chain.

At the time, if you had looked up *trade unionist* in the dictionary, you would have found a picture of Kevin Corporon next to the words. Committed and passionate about what he believed, Corporon worked endlessly to emancipate literally thousands of female service workers from the corporate union they'd been lured into joining. The campaign literature that Kevin handed out to those who were willing to accept them condemned the current union for its lack of democracy and its lack of representation.

"Communication with members is essential to a strong and united union," he said. Workers were entitled to a decent honest union, and the United Food and Commercial Workers was just that kind of union.

Kevin believed with every fiber of his being that unions carried the obligation of communicating to their members about matters that would affect them.

Kevin failed at the time because of the actions of one Cliff Evans, an upwardly mobile union official. Cliff would eventually take control of the Canadian UFCW. Kevin Corporon soft-landed with

UFCW Local 1000a. The local had its origins as an employee association (Union of Canadian Retail Employees) that represented workers at Loblaws supermarkets starting in the 1940s. In the late 1970s, UCRE's president, Dan Gilbert, merged his union with what would become the UFCW.

The passionate, committed trade unionist that Kevin Corporon was would soon evolve into the corporate unionist that he had, not too long ago, heatedly criticized. It happened when he became president of UFCW Local 1000a.

The champion of the female service workers, who had preached that communication was essential for a membership, subsequently spouted that the membership could not be trusted with even the simplest decisions. The union had too many complicated contracts to negotiate, too many significant funds to manage, and many labor-management dealings to foster. If democracy was allowed, a member who didn't understand the intricacies could do serious damage. Kevin had been appointed to his position of president by his predecessor and was not democratically elected by the membership.

"That's how we do things in our union," he explained to a member.

How things were done in his union has worked well for him. As president of UFCW Local 1000a, which represents over twenty thousand service industry workers across Ontario, Corporon did quite well. Although at the time his members were earning a little over seven dollars an hour, he was taking home a generous salary and benefits package that totaled just over $146,000 a year. Although his ability to negotiate a contract seems to be questionable, Kevin will never have to worry about being removed through a democratic process. The UFCW Canada doesn't have one.

Corporon's backroom deals would put a lobbyist to shame.

At the heart of the deal was the Loblaw Companies. The profitable company was given the ability to hire cheaper labor at a new chain of stores in order to give UFCW Local 1000a thousands of new members, which equated to a nice rich revenue stream for Corporon to tap into.

With this new sweet deal, UFCW took concession bargaining to a whole new level: the gutter.

According to documents filed by Loblaw and UFCW Local 1000a with the Ontario Labour Relations Board, this how the two sides came up with their anti-employee agreement: Sometime in 2002, senior executives of Loblaw Companies met with UFCW officials Kevin Corporon from Local 1000a, Wayne Hanley from Local 175, Brian Williamson from Local 1977, and UFCW Canada Director Mike Fraser. It was at this meeting that the Loblaw executives informed the UFCW officials that Wal-Mart was coming to town with its Sam's Club warehouse stores and its Walmart Supercenters.

In response to the competition that Loblaw Companies expected to face, the company had developed a business strategy to make it more competitive. It would establish a chain of new stores, called Real Canadian Super Stores (RCSSs), which would sell groceries and some department store merchandise, sort of like Walmart Supercenter stores in the United States.

Because Loblaw had already established a brand name with Canadian shoppers, the new chain would also carry the banners of the corporation's better known entities, such as Fortino's and Zehr's.

In doing so, however, that would mean the RCSSs would automatically be absorbed under the current bargaining agreement with UFCW locals. Loblaw wanted to compete with Walmart and therefore believed that they would need to lower the wages and benefits of the new employees of the new Loblaws supercenters. So Loblaw executives put forth a proposal to the officials from the UFCW: in exchange for several hundreds, possibly thousands, of new members paying dues, the UFCW would agree to a lower wage and a cheaper benefits package.

The unspoken word was that the UFCW could agree or Loblaw would open without the brand names and leave the UFCW out in the cold, where it would lose that additional revenue stream. According to Kevin Corporon, Loblaw also threatened to close unionized stores, which would create many unemployed union members.

According to Loblaw, that was not an accurate statement about what was discussed at the meeting. Threatening to close down union establishments as a retaliatory measure violates Canadian labor law.

The UFCW, without taking a time-out to consider the issue presented before them, agreed to a deal that would have an adverse effect on their current members.

It took several months to negotiate the finer points of their clandestine agreement. Then sometime in June 2003, the deal was done. The "scope" clauses of the UFCW locals' current contracts were be amended to include workers from the RCSSs. A substantial number of new requirements that would apply to the new members were added to the existing contracts. RCSS workers would have different wage rates and different entitlements to benefits, overtime, vacations, hours of work, statutory holiday pay, and bereavement leave. In addition, some jobs that were in the bargaining unit at existing stores would be nonunion at the new RCSSs, thereby giving management greater flexibility in managing.

The whole sinister plot was engaged in because of the threat of Wal-Mart coming to town. Poor Wal-Mart—the union blames it for everything; it's the George W. Bush of the retail world. However, the poor, put-upon, threatened UFCW managed to scrape out a meager payoff of $450,000 to each of the UFCW locals over three years. Nothing for the members who were the recipients of the concessions. Good to know that the UFCW was able to take care of UFCW Inc., though.

The UFCW claims it was acting in the interests of the members—members who were never given the chance to vote on the new arrangement. With friends like that, who needs enemies? The UFCW claims that the terms from Loblaw forbade the union from giving the members an opportunity to ratify the deal. OK, let me see if I understand this: the UFCW, which is supposed to represent the employees at their place of employment, actually took its marching orders from their members' employer. I don't think it is this is how this union representation thing is supposed to work.

UFCW members were outraged when they found out that the company didn't want them to have an opportunity to vote and that their union agreed to it. The union pleaded with its members to understand that if it had allowed them to vote on the arrangement, Loblaw would have taken the substandard offer off the table, and UFCW officials couldn't let that happen. After all, there was $450,000 on the table for selling their members into an inferior contract. Let's not lose sight of what was really important to UFCW Inc.

UFCW officials insisted that this was all for the members' benefit, that the members were just too simpleminded to understand the great deal they were just handed.

While the UFCW members might be simpleminded, they were able to grasp what their intellectually superior representatives could not—when you give up wages and benefits in a contract, that is a concession, not a win. Threatening to close stores to retaliate against the union for not agreeing to the concessions is against the law, and if it was the win that UFCW officials claimed, why did Loblaw threaten the union to begin with? The members were far from celebrating their victory; they were in shock. Their union was telling them it had not bargained concessions by agreeing to a reduction in wages and benefits.

Of course, even Canada has a media that is selective about what they splash across their pages in a negative manner. Most mainstream media outlets would only print the news releases from UFCW and Loblaw. In fact the mainstream media described how UFCW members were sacrificing in order to be on the frontlines in the war against Wal-Mart. The UFCW wrapped everything in up in warlike terms, such as "The Wal-Mart Invasion," "The Wal-Mart Threat," and who could forget the all-time favorite, "titans pitched in battle"—and the Canadian mainstream media printed it. I honestly am starting to have sympathy pains for Wal-Mart at this point.

One UFCW member who started a blog posted this: "We half expect to see Saddam Hussein himself crossing Lake Ontario into the Canadian market carrying a banner 'Low Prices Always' flying from the end of his upraised rifle."

However, the *Toronto Star* and *Now Magazine* did take up the call from members and reported on the secret deal between UFCW and Loblaw. Their reporting revealed a less-than-flattering picture of what UFCW did to its members.

Cliff Evans's nephew, UFCW Canada Director Mike Fraser, called it a "forward-thinking accord." With forward thinking like that, it is amazing that companies aren't clamoring for a union at their sites. After all, the UFCW did more for Loblaw profits than the customers did.

While the UFCW members made the sacrifice in the great Wal-Mart War, the union profited from the battle. The union's take from its war-profiteering ways came to a grand total of $1.35 million! I wonder what Wal-Mart would think if it ever found out that it was to blame for the union adding over a million dollars to its coffers. Oh, the irony!

Of course the Wal-Mart invasion never occurred; the two retail giants never engaged in a battle to the death for a slice of the retail market; and to the relief of the one UFCW blogger, Saddam Hussein never landed on Canadian shores. In fact not only did it not take place, but according to Wal-Mart, the company never had plans to bring their supercenters to Canada. Wal-Mart only had four Sam's Clubs slated to open in Toronto to compete with Costco.

I wonder if those UFCW members can get their dues back.

Chapter 9
Secret SEIU Negotiations Spark Protests

And now, from the great state of California, we bring "SEIU and the Secret Deal Part Deux!"

In April 2009, SEIU decide to impose a top-down contract on its members of the National Union of Healthcare Workers. SEIU, for some reason, shies away from the bright light of transparency and prefers to deliver its members into subjugation through a more clandestine method. The settlement that SEIU negotiated would affect hundreds of nursing-home workers in Northern California.

This time SEIU decided to conduct its dastardly deeds with a new partner—the for-profit Foresight Management Services. The new contract would apply to employees at seven of the nursing-home facilities. SEIU-NUHW leaders had been fighting against this type of underhanded dealing before being put into trusteeship. In fact, for those thousands of rank-and-file members, the whole scenario being played out by SEIU International emphasized the division that existed between the International and its members—a division created by one side with a strong belief in the democratic process (NUHW) and the other side (SEIU), which believed in a form of corporate unionism: do not ask what your union can do for you, but what sacrifice you can make to fill the coffers of your union.

As the plot thickens, the truth of the pathetic sellout of the union's membership starts to be revealed, and the following facts come to light.

The workers of the nursing home elected a bargaining committee to represent them in the negotiations. At the beginning of the weekend, twenty of those bargaining committee members arrived in Oakland, California, at the union's local office. Contract negotiation meetings were already scheduled with the company, Foresight Management Services. Before the scheduled meeting, another negotiation session took place, at which time the elected members of the negotiation committee rejected the company's offer specifically where it concerned wages and benefits. The current proposal from Foresight had much lower wages and benefits than the criteria set by other SEIU-NUHW nursing-home workers' collective bargaining agreements. Because of the impasse encountered at the previous negotiations, the negotiating committee, on behalf of the workers who had elected them, terminated the temporary extension of the expired contract and began preparations for a strike.

At this point everything was proceeding as it would in any ordinary union negotiation. When hitting an impasse, unions take strike votes and prepare to initiate the only leverage they have when negotiating with an employer. Then something went wrong. Horribly, unexpectedly wrong. When the bargaining committee arrived that Friday, SEIU Executive Vice President Mary Kay Henry and other SEIU leaders greeted them. Without warning or provocation, the democratically elected committee members were prohibited from attending the negotiations. SEIU leaders actually locked them out of the union's local office and left them standing out front on the public sidewalk.

Why did SEIU do this? Well because they are the voice of the workers...in fact, according to SEIU organizers, the workers are the union.

Ah, no. Wrong answer. Read on.

SEIU leadership conveniently suffered a bout of amnesia, forgot that they were the workers' voice—a union of the workers—and began talking with company officials about a contract that would benefit the union. Imagine that! With some handpicked members who were not elected to the delegating committee, SEIU commenced negotiating. The few members who were selected to attend represented only three of the seven nursing homes, which meant the workers in the other four nursing homes suffered from extreme laryngitis brought on by the self-serving officials of SEIU.

When SEIU members found out about the dastardly deed committed by SEIU and their handpicked yes-men, a petition of no confidence in the negotiating committee was passed around and signed by over 70 percent of the membership.

However, strangely, the SEIU elitists ignored their working-class members and left them out on the streets and sidewalks. Using tactics that were normally reserved just for employers, members picketed the union offices, and soon the press started to arrive. With TV stations and newspapers gathering to report the story, SEIU officials moved fast. When they invited the duly elected, but deposed, negotiating committee inside, the committee members felt that a battle had been won, and they would now participate in their own talks with their employer.

Not so fast, you little insignificant dues-paying members! Corralling the legitimate negotiating committee members into a small room, SEIU informed them that if they wanted to participate in the fun with the employers' negotiations, they must sign a loyalty oath to SEIU's leaders and also rescind their signatures on NLRB petitions requesting to join NUHW. Wait a minute—didn't they take an oath when they originally joined SEIU, as its constitution (book of arcane rules and ridiculous pledges) stated they must. Yes, but we want another loyalty oath, and a pinkie pledge, too! (I just made up the pinkie pledge part.)

The legitimate bargaining committee was disturbed and distraught by the actions of these protectors of the working class from big bad bosses, and carried their pissed-off butts back to the sidewalk, where they continued picketing and chanting for many hours. After a lengthy time, they left; but then hours later they flexed their muscle by sending those usurpers of workers' right a strong message. They served their employers with a ten-day notice of intent to strike at every one of the seven nursing homes.

Never let it be said that SEIU could be bullied by its own members into representing them properly. Under the gun, now that the workers had issued an intent to strike, SEIU accepted the company proposal that the membership had turned down in January. The substandard contract gave the employees a 30 percent lower economic package than other SEIU-NUHW nursing home workers whose local union was not in trusteeship.

Knowing that to put this contract before the membership would only result in the contract proposal being voted down, SEIU officials felt they had to be a little tricky in how members voted on the contract proposal to ensure passage.

SEIU knew that the trick to getting the secret sellout contract passed was to curtail membership participation, so they neglected to provide advance notice to members as to when and where the voting would take place. SEIU officials then distorted the realities of the proposed contract.

Now, even with no advanced notice, word got around, and members showed up to vote. Knowing that letting the members vote on their contract would not be in the best interest of SEIU, officials decided to bar great numbers of their members from even casting a ballot. Therefore, when a worker arrived to vote, SEIU would tell the member that the polls had closed. A really wicked form of voter suppression. Not bad, of course—they did have practice with tricky voting during the 2008 election.

Just to make sure there was no possible way this contract could be voted down, SEIU delivered the coup de grace by refusing to allow any member to witness the ballots being counted, which is a common practice in any union.

It did not take long for a petition to surface that the members started to circulate. The petition demanded that SEIU re-vote the ratification of the bargaining agreement in the standard democratic manner, with full revelation of all of the terms of SEIU's substandard agreement. Given SEIU's overbearing and arrogant manner, many members believe that union officials stuffed the ballot box so they could ratify a substandard contract that would be celebrated by the company and rejected by the union's own members.

What happened to the union belonging to the members?

Chapter 10

Can You Hear Me Now? Members Abandoned as Unions Side with Verizon

In 2009, a group of workers, members of the Communications Workers of America (CWA) and International Brotherhood of Electrical Workers (IBEW), found themselves on the receiving end of the wrath of their employer, Verizon. To add insult to injury, the workers' own unions sided with the employer. In what can only be classified as abandonment, members of the CWA and the IBEW found out what happens when their union has a different agenda than its members.

The betrayal of striking members all started when forty-five thousand striking workers were ordered back to work, ending their two-week strike. Those forty-five thousand members must have been sickened, going out on strike, thinking they had the full weight of their unions behind them, only to discover too late that their unions were placing their full weight *on* their own members. During the strike, Verizon fired many striking workers, and as expected the union filed charges and threatened the company with further work stoppages...Oh, wait a minute, that isn't what happened.

Yes, Verizon fired workers who struck the company, but the CWA and IBEW...well, they didn't think that was a battle worth fighting for, so they instructed their members to return to work—those who still had a job—and when they got around to it, they would examine the evidence that Verizon had compiled against the fired employees. No demands for reinstatement, no unfair labor-practice charges. The unions did absolutely nothing to defend or protect those members who found themselves on the outside looking in.

The Verizon employees affected were acknowledged as very outspoken, even militant, by those who knew them. Some said the termination of these employees was as much in the two unions' interest as it was in the employer's. The CWA and IBEW wanted them made an example of since at times they were just as critical of the unions, and the unions wanted a more malleable membership. The top union officials wanted the membership to see an example of what could happen if they didn't toe the line of the union officials' prattle.

The return-to-work order unequivocally states: "Disputes involving disciplinary actions arising from employee conduct that occurred between and including August 7, 2011, and the Return to Work Date are not subject to the arbitration provisions" of the contract. This sacrificed the striking workers' right to fight any terminations that Verizon chose to enact on those workers. Verizon was given free rein to institute the ultimate punishment, with no help from their union for those affected.

The unions also conceded any deadline for the collection of evidence against the employees engaged in the strike and a timeline of when the employer would present evidence to the unions. Any workers caught up in the investigative net would not be paid, would not be able to defend themselves, and would not have any right to view any evidence collected against them to mount their own defense.

A union promises its members that it will be the defenders of their rights, that it will stand between them and the abuses of a corporate America that doesn't see a person, only profit and loss. I don't blame Verizon for the travesty these workers experienced; rather, I do think the unions should be held accountable for the negligence they promoted toward the very members they were supposed to protect. At least eighty workers were thrown under the bus by their representing unions. With representation like that, why have a contract at all? Just what were those workers the unions took to the streets fighting for?

Members who had to return to work felt guilt at having a job, while those who fought hard were denied the right to return. Some even stated in interviews that it was wrong to abandon these co-workers to the political collaboration that took place between the company and the two unions. Union officials tried to reassure those members who still had jobs that everything would work out just fine, but to most, it didn't feel that way. Instead, most of the membership believed they had had Verizon "on their knees," that Verizon was not able to carry on its business, and that they should not have gone back to work unless all forty-five thousand striking members went back to work.

Although most accepted the reality that thousands of workers would not walk off the job to support the few who'd lost their jobs, they felt that the union could have fought harder. They felt that with Verizon backed into a corner, the CWA and IBEW could have negotiated a return to work for all employees, or at least due process for those who were fired—but the unions did neither. Some members expressed on Facebook and other social media outlets that they were not happy about their unions caving in and failing to represent all workers equally. They felt those who were suspended or fired were "screwed." As one worker pointed out, "The company will hold them hostage until Sept 30, that is the date that they said they hope to have all disciplinary matters resolved by. So that would be two months with no pay, not a victory in my eyes."

The sad part is that while they were negotiating the contract prior to the strike vote, the unions were ginning up the membership, agitating the workforce so that a strike could be a realistic threat to the company, and then, when they got the workers all riled up, they threw them under the bus!

Both the IBEW and CWA claimed that they had vanquished Verizon...slapped them silly...forced Verizon to "refocus bargaining and narrow the issues," a victory of David over Goliath. Verizon's top executives, however, have a different take on the outcome of all this chaos. They instead point to the obvious, which is that none of the major issues were removed from the negotiating table.

After engaging in a strike that semi-paralyzed the wireless giant, IBEW and CWA eagerly rushed in to snatch defeat from the jaws of victory, starting concessionary bargaining even before all the picket signs were put away. Perhaps they didn't want to pay strike pay to forty-five thousand people. Or worse yet, those forty-five thousand people wouldn't be able to pay their dues if they languished on the strike line for too long. Whatever the reasons, the two unions made a speedy retreat, while the company itself did not retreat from its original objective of cutting pensions and health care and eliminating work rules.

"We remain committed to our objectives," said Marc Reed, Verizon's executive vice president of human resources. "We look forward to negotiating the important issues that are integral to the future health of Verizon's wire line business."

Many claimed that Verizon was victimizing its workers, but the real villain was the unions. The company is in business to make a profit, and though you may want to argue ethics or the moral ground, those don't really play here. Verizon has an obligation to its stockholders and is fulfilling it to the best of its ability. In other words, the company is doing what it was created to do. End of story on Verizon's culpability. But where are the ethics and the moral ground of the unions? They are the ones who pledged to be the great defenders of the working class. They are the ones who took their members' money and promised to slay the corporate dragons. Verizon did what it was created to do; the unions didn't.

When an institution created to protect working people fails or no longer chooses to pursue that mission statement, what is the purpose of its existence anymore? It was the unions' responsibility, due diligence, to demand evidence from Verizon on behalf of the accused members. It was the unions' responsibility to conduct a separate investigation in defense of those workers. Why didn't they?

The charges lodged against those workers resulted in the courts granting injunctions and the involvement of law enforcement in the form of both local police officers and FBI agents. Strikers were accused of vandalism and sabotage—where was their defense? Why did the unions who represented these people bail? Many workers believed they had been singled out because of their aggressive stance in the face of the strike: attempting to block people from crossing the picket line to work in the positions the strikers had walked away from.

As one worker and union member was reported to have posted, "How could we let this happen??"

Chapter 11
UAW's Dear John Letter

I could have written this story using my own words, but when I stumbled on a speech by a man who was there and involved in Accuride, I felt that he deserved the chance to tell this story to a different audience in his own words. It's over a decade later, but it doesn't lessen the hurt from the betrayal these people encountered from their union, the UAW.

The following is a speech by Brother Billy Robinson, president of UAW Local 2036, to the Workers Democracy Network, in Oakland, California, on November 11, 2000.

Accuride is the foremost maker of steel truck wheels in the world. We supply 80 percent of the market for steel truck wheels, one ton or larger. We have two plants; one in Henderson, Kentucky, and one in London, Ontario.

On February 20, 1998, our Local went on strike, voting 371 to 9 to reject the contract proposed by Accuride. The contract had language stating: no person or classification has a right to any certain job. It also gave the company the unilateral and unrestricted right to subcontract any work. They said they were going to subcontract ALL the skilled trades work.

Accuride wouldn't even agree to anti-discrimination language. We even went down to language that simply said, "We'll comply with the law." But it wasn't good enough for them.

The strike was authorized by the UAW International Executive Board and our Regional Director, who at the time was Ron Gettlefinger. The UAW controls 95% of the plants we supply. We thought the UAW would use its clout. Just 120 miles from our plant, in Louisville, there's a Ford truck plant with 13,000 UAW members. If the UAW leadership had spread the word in that plant, "Those are scab wheels," our strike would have been over in less than four weeks. If they told workers at Navistar, Mack, Peterbilt, and GM Truck & Bus, "Those are scab wheels you're putting on that truck," our strike would've been over in no time.

In March of 1998 we voted to go back to work unconditionally. Accuride paid people from my Local $4,000 each to cross the picket line. 29 out of 439 members crossed the picket line by the latter part of March. The strike wasn't working. On March 30, 1998, I told the members, "We've got to end the strike; go back to work; we'll work to rule; we'll do what we have to do."

Before we could even take that vote, Accuride locked us out. The membership voted overwhelmingly to return to work, and 354 to 9 to reject the contract. That was two contracts that the membership, by the end of March, had rejected because of union busting language.

In September of 1998, they put another proposal on the table. They said the Bargaining Committee of the Local Union was misleading the members, not telling them what the contract really said. They claimed we were pressuring people, and not getting an accurate vote.

So I went down to the Catholic church—they have a big auditorium—and convinced them to let us use it. We set it up with loudspeakers. The vote was by secret ballot. The International Rep was there from day one. There wasn't a period, a comma, or anything that went into those proposals, or into those meetings, that the International Rep didn't approve.

At that meeting in September 1998, we presented a proposal to the membership from the company. This contract contained the same language; unilateral right to subcontract any work, and no person or classification has the right to any certain job, but this time they put another little kicker in there. They had the unilateral and unrestricted right to alter, amend, modify, change, or delete the pension program, at will. And the unilateral and unrestricted right to alter, amend, modify, change, or delete any out-of-pocket premiums or coverage in the insurance.

We presented it to the membership. The membership rejected it overwhelmingly. We had 17 people guarding the ballot boxes. Everyone was double-checked and triple-checked to ensure they only had one ballot. The International Rep was there to oversee it. When it was over the International Rep said, "You will not vote on another proposal until there has been a significant change." Our members said, "OK, by God, we're going to stand by that."

From day one, the company was ready to recognize the UAW as the exclusive bargaining agent of all employees, but we had absolutely no rights on the shop floor. There was no mention of a president, a union steward, or anything else in the language. If you wanted to file a grievance, you would have to do it after work on your own time. If a supervisor started hitting on a sister working in the plant, and if she said she wanted a steward, the supervisor could say, "it's not a matter of importance" and she wouldn't get a steward.

This is the type of language they kept throwing at us. Every time we voted, it got progressively worse. For the next year, we refused to vote on anything. We told the company publicly, "Shove it up your ass until you've changed it."

On August 14, 1999, I was called at home. It was a Saturday afternoon. I was told to get my Executive Board together and to meet the International Rep at the union hall. I said, "Look, this is Saturday afternoon. This just can't happen." He said, "I'm not asking you, I'm telling you." I said, "OK, if you put it that way." So I started calling my officers.

Let me tell you, people, I've been with the UAW 23 years. I've been union ever since I was 17 years old. My grandaddy sat on the front porch sipping moonshine with John L. Lewis up in Eastern Kentucky in the coal mines. All my family is union. He called my officers in that day and told me that as of the last day of August, the UAW would no longer provide economic support for this Local.

I said, "What does that mean? What are you saying?"

He said, "As of the last day of August, you won't have any strike insurance, you won't have any strike pay. The International is not going to pull your charter. You'll still remain on the picket line. They're not ending the strike/lock-out."

I looked at him and I said, "You're joking."

He said, "No, I've been instructed to come here and tell you that." He said, "I've never seen it happen, but it's exactly what I've come to tell you now."

My officers looked at me and said, "What do you think?" I got the Regional Director, Terry Thurman, on the phone. He said, "Tell them to go back to work." How the hell can I tell them to go back to work when we've been locked out for 18 months? He wanted us to go tell the company, "We've lost our benefits now, so you've got to take us back."

The Executive Board agreed we needed to call a special membership meeting. We held it in the parking lot of the union hall. I told my members:

"This is the saddest day of my life. I feel like the guts have been pulled out of me. I can tell you today that what Accuride couldn't accomplish, the

UAW International has done in one fell swoop. They've deserted you. As of today, you will no longer have any economic support from the International."

Then we took another secret ballot vote about whether we were going to vote on the contract or not. The members said, "The hell with the UAW. We came out here for a reason. We're going to stick together. We're not going back until we get what we came out for. They can take their strike benefits and shove 'em. We'll stay on this picket line till hell freezes over." Well, I haven't seen Satan up there yet, but it feels cold enough to freeze hell quite often.

I had been an organizer for the UAW for 15 or 16 months when the strike started. I've been all over that part of the country down there. I was involved in salting Toyota in Princeton, Indiana, a new plant. [Salting: to help get pro-union workers hired at a nonunion plant to aid the organizing effort.]

I had helped get about 600 people hired into that plant. Everybody in that part of the country had heard me tell how great the UAW was, how democratic the process was in the UAW. The people turned around and looked at me and said, "What happened?" But there was one thing that I knew from my experience in being a president, and being an organizer, and being a union member. I firmly believe the tenet that when anybody reaches out for help, the unions need to be there. That's what unions are for. During the organizing drives, I would tell people, "What is the union? You are. Read the Constitution of the United States. It says We the People, in order to form a more perfect union..."

Well, that day in the parking lot, August 28, 1999, I found out exactly what a union is.

In October 1999, Accuride came out with yet another proposal. It was even worse, if you can imagine that. The membership voted it down by secret ballot. That was the fifth time. People were getting tired. They'd been out there over a year and a half, but they voted it down again. I was catching flack from everywhere. People would say, "We thought we gave you a mandate that unless there's a tentative agreement approved by the Bargaining Committee, not to bring it back for a vote." I understood, but all this time had gone by, and the publicity was eating us alive. So I had them vote again on it. And sure enough, they voted it down again.

After the International cut off our strike benefits, I told the members, "There's one thing you have to do. You have to communicate. You've got to go out and tell other union members what's going on. So I want every one of you to leave here today, and to get on that Internet. I want everybody to know what the International leadership has done."

I got one member who sent out 3,000 e-mails in the next week. You wouldn't believe how many e-mails we got in answer. We got them from Puerto Rico, from Ireland, England, Australia, and all over the United States. People just couldn't believe what we were telling them. We put out tremendous amounts of literature.

I took about 40 members and went to Louisville. At midnight we hand billed the plant when they were changing shifts. I talked with people who actually put the wheels on the vehicles. I told them, "Don't listen to anything someone else tells you. I'm here to tell you now, I'm the guy who sat at the table. I'm the guy who told your president and your bargaining chair in this plant over a year ago what was going on." The workers didn't have any idea that they were putting on scab wheels. Nobody on the shop floor did.

We went out in the community, too. You can ask an old farmer out in the fields who's never been union in his life, did they vote on a contract? And he'd be able to tell you, "you're damn right they did, five times, and they rejected it five times."

UAW International leaders were fit to be tied about what we did, and are still doing. Now, they are going to say that I've been talking to an "anti-union group" here. That's the b.s. they're spreading all over the place. Any time you talk to a group that does not endorse the opinions of the International officers, you're anti-union. Well, I've got news for you. On August 28, those members told me what a union was. They said, "It's us. We're here. We came out for a reason. We're going to stick together."

President Yokich didn't like that too much. We did not go away. UAW International leaders have said that I'm a renegade, that I belong to some communist group, and all we are down here in Local 2036 is a big bunch of Ku Klux Klan people. Let me tell you something. One of my Bargaining Committee people is black. A homosexual is head of our Women's Committee. Three of our Trustees are black. They all say to me, "We're coming in wearing sheets next week." We looked at it as a joke.

But this is how the International tries to shut you up. If the brother over there says something critical of the leadership, they're going to say something

*personally detrimental about him. But you can't let that affect you. You've got
to laugh it off and go on. You've got to communicate.*

[Union and progressive tactic: if you can't attack the message,
attack the messenger.]

*I'll go anywhere that anybody wants me to, and I'll tell them what's
happening. I've got every copy of every proposal. I've got every letter that
was written. In March of 1998, I wrote the International to ask them for a
corporate campaign against Accuride. I sent them a list of the customers, and
a bunch of handbills that I wanted to put out. I wanted to hit every truck stop
in the country. You see what happened to Firestone. We were going to go to the
truck stops and tell them about the scab wheels that were on the trucks. They
refused to let us do it.*

*In March of '98 I still thought, well, they're going to do something,
they're going to help us out some way or another. But in August of '99 I found
out they weren't going to do a damn thing. So we did it ourselves. They didn't
have to put out any handbills for us. I know how to write them. I know how
to get my point across. We're still doing it.*

*Well, by May of 2000, a lot of people across the country had been getting
a hold of me. The first people who came to our picket line, after they took our
benefits away, were the "Blue Shirts" out of the Caterpillar plant in Peoria,
Ill. I've got some of their shirts and I wear them proudly. You've got to earn
these shirts. You don't just buy them.*

*Let me tell you about these people. They took on Vance Security at Cat-
erpillar. They still haven't given up. These guys, right to this day, are still in
there fighting because Shoemaker sold them out. The International gave the
scabs $100,000 a piece to settle a bogus harassment lawsuit, and let them work
next to UAW members who walked the line. Then Yokich and Shoemaker
called it a victory.*

*Bill Wheats and the Blue Shirts were the first people on our picket line
after the International cut off our benefits. They came in with money just before Christmas 1999. They asked, what do you need? They told us the tactics
they had used in their strike because we had Vance Security at Accuride, too.
Vance came in a month before the contract expired. They were ready for us.
They intended to put us out on the street.*

*You've got to use whatever means are available to you, because it's a
war. We started getting e-mails, letters, and visits from a lot of people, and I*

started finding out, we aren't the only ones. There's a whole lot of people across this country just like us.

Larry Solomon from Caterpillar came to see us. Mike Griffin from the War Zone Foundation out of Decatur. Hawk Wright and Gene Austin, out of Local 594, Pontiac, Michigan. Socialist Workers out of Chicago. The Workers Democracy Network. All these people started visiting our union hall, asking, "What do you need?" Running articles in their papers. Spreading our story all over the country. I started getting e-mails from everywhere. As soon as they cut off our benefits, we sent people to Detroit to picket Solidarity House. We thought people needed to know. ABC News picked it up and ran it all over the country. We went back to Detroit in May 2000. We brought a lot of diverse groups together and we picketed Solidarity House again.

UAW President Steve Yokich didn't like that we rejected his instructions and proceeded to do what we had to do. In April of 2000, I received a notice from the International to attend a hearing in Detroit. The letter claimed that the local's existence was "threatened" because we had not bargained in a "prudent and realistic way," hadn't held "secret ballot votes," and for other "unspecified reasons."

Region 3 Director, Terry Thurman, said we needed an administrator to "restore the democratic process" in our local. They sent word throughout the UAW that it was an "unauthorized strike." Yet Gettlefinger told me three times, on February 20, "Take em out."

At the hearing that I attended in April 2000, I had all the information. I put before the International leaders all the dates, times, and figures of every secret ballot vote that we had on the contract. They sent us in and out of the room four or five times.

Finally, Reuben Burks looked at me and said, "Billy, we have a problem. Maybe you can help us with it." I said, OK, what is it? He said, "All these handbills, all these e-mails, and web sites, and all these things criticizing Mr. Yokich are putting him in a bad light. Maybe you can help us make these go away." I presumed these were the "unspecified reasons." I said, let me answer your question with a statement.

I told him how long I'd been union, and how I had professed that the UAW was the greatest union that ever was all over that part of the country. I said if we did something wrong, we know how to take our punishment. But we want to know why you took our benefits away from us.

Yokich looked at me and said, "I don't give a damn how many e-mails you put out, how many web sites you put up, we're the most powerful union around, and you aren't going to bother me, and you're not the first ones we've cut off." I've got that remark in a transcript.

People couldn't believe it. He never gave me an answer. He said, "We're going to place you under an administrator—a friendly administrator." I looked up and said, just exactly what is a "friendly administrator"? "Don't worry about it," he said. "Just go on back down there, and hold your meetings and do what you always do. Just don't worry about it." He said, "We'll make our decision on May 8."

I thought to myself, May 8, huh? He's got the damn handbill about the rally on May 8 right in front of him. He knows I'm going to be in front of Solidarity House when he makes that decision. He was right. I stood in front of his car when he came out of the gate.

They placed us under an administrator. They came in and took all our books, our financial records, and our checking account. Wanted to choke us to death. Or so they thought. We got them back now. We had already opened up another account, the Henderson Workers Solidarity Fund. Our thanks to Local 594 out of Pontiac, Michigan. They did a bucket shake at the gates and collected $7,100. We put that in our account. That's how I'm here today.

Fellow workers, we have got to promote solidarity all across this country. All of us. It's our responsibility. If there's somebody that doesn't know what a union is, you need to organize them, you need to explain to them why they need a union. You're probably going to have to go back into your own local and organize your own local, because they don't know what a union is.

By October 2000 I'd been all over the place, talking with everybody that I could talk to. I was scheduled into Kokomo, Indiana, UAW Local 685, for a meeting with some UAW members up there. They asked me to come up and give a talk. I said, no problem, I'll be up there. They asked me to come up October 4. Okay. It's about a five and a half hour drive. They put it into the newspapers that I was going to speak there.

Terry Thurman, the Director of Region 3, where I'm from, was sitting in the union hall 10 minutes away, hiding. He wouldn't come around when I was speaking. But he called my officers, told them they had to meet him in Indianapolis, but I wasn't invited. I said, that's all right, I got to be in Kokomo anyway, it's not a problem. I told them to call me the minute they got out of *the meeting and tell me what it was all about. He told my officers they were reinstating our benefits on October 5, with all the insurance, and double strike pay, $350 a week.*

So I went into that meeting at Local 685 in Kokomo, and I told them, yeah, they gave us our benefits back. But I haven't seen the strings on it yet. I haven't heard the reason yet. There are 14 months unanswered for, when we didn't have any strike pay, when we didn't have any insurance.

I've got a member who's 62 years old now. When we came out, he had $40,000 in the bank; he had already paid his home off; he owned everything he had. He was looking forward to putting two more years in so he could retire. Two months after they canceled our benefits, he had a heart attack and a quadruple bypass surgery. He had to refinance his house to pay the bills. He's $87,000 in debt right now. And now they come and want to give us our benefits back.

I've got another lady that I'm trying to help get social security. For 14 months she didn't have the money to buy her medicine, so she didn't take any medicine. She's on the verge of dying right now. We've had two suicides, and I don't know how many broken marriages. It's unbelievable what so many people went through. But we've still got over 300 people on the picket line right now. Most of them don't figure they'll go back to work.

The majority say, "By God, we aren't going back, but we aren't giving up. We're going to stay out here." They gave us our benefits back October 5th. It's been six weeks now. Anyone who was forced into retirement like myself, won't get anything.

Before, if you had some reason you couldn't pick up your strike pay, it'd be no problem. I'd just have it written out, and I'd be around the union hall working, and you'd just come by when you could, and I'd give it to you. Or your wife would come in, or your husband, there'd be no problem.

Since the International took over, you've got to be there in person to pick that check up. It started out 9 am to 4 pm that you could pick it up. Then they changed it to 9 am to 2 pm. So the people who get off at 3:30 couldn't get there. Now it's even worse than that. It's only 9 am to 1 pm. And I'm going to have to tell the members next week that the International's going to audit us again.

You've got to come down to the office and bring any records of earnings you've got into the hall. They're going to do everything they can to try to find us dirty. So they gave us our benefits back. But that's because we took them on. When they told us to go away, we said "no."

In negotiations, September 18 and 19, the Deputy Director of Region 3 was sent in to be the spokesman and direct negotiations. He came in real proud. He said, "I got a contract." Now, this was just two minutes before the company people came in.

The first thing I looked for in that contract was the article that stated salary people had the right to bump hourly people off the floor. I have people with 25 years' seniority that would have to stay out on the street and let a 5 year salary person take their job. Soon as I looked, there it was. He was going to present this to the company as a union proposal. I told him, Gary, if that's in the contract, don't come on union property with it; the members will kill you! Even people who told me they wanted to vote for the contract said, "As long as it has that language we're not going to vote on it. Period."

So he sends one of the Bargaining Committee members over to the store to buy some black markers so he can mark it out. It was obvious as soon as he started presenting it to the company that he'd never read it. He didn't have a damn clue what was in it. His secretary went and got a grievance procedure out of another contract from another plant, and just copied it verbatim and put it in there.

Nothing in the language fit our Local. It talked about the plant Chair-person. Well, we don't have a Chairperson. I'm the President, and by my of-fice I sit on the Bargaining Committee. I head all committees. None of that language fit. Before they took our strike benefits away from us, we had 24 articles signed off. We don't have anything now. Zero.

This is the type of leadership that the UAW had sent to help us negotiate a fair contract. The company people just laughed at him.

When we went on strike Accuride was owned by Phelps Dodge. The attorney who's been responsible for breaking 80 percent of the unions at Phelps Dodge is the one we're negotiating with. We still are. This guy is an idiot, but he's good at his job. He'll sit there, and he'll talk on a subject until you're almost asleep. He gets $1,400 an hour. He doesn't give a damn how long he stays at the table.

The UAW is still there. We got our benefits back. That was just a small battle. The war's still out there. And it's up to every one of us to continue the fight, continue to build solidarity, so we can come together, and get rid of all this petty stuff—like the IBEW Local 1701 crossing our picket line every day. They have for over a year.

We've also got pipe fitters and millwrights crossing our picket line. We've got so many people who don't care, because they have forgotten or don't know what solidarity is or what a union is.

Two weeks ago I attended a meeting in Flint, Michigan, and we founded the "UAW Solidarity Coalition." We're going to go out and try to bring in as many UAW people as we can into this Coalition.

In Lansing, Michigan, the retirees from UAW Concern got a hold of people in the plant. They were doing a food drive for our Local. They have a big union hall and it was full of food. But the Local officers told them, "Get it out of here now, or we'll call the Salvation Army and have them come and get it. We're not supporting those people in Local 2036." Last Christmas at Peterbilt in Madison, Tennessee, the people adopted a bunch of our members and donated truckloads of food. Really did a good deed. But then the International told them, you'd better not do this. Now I can't even get them to answer my letters.

At Local 594, the leadership did everything they could to stop that fund-raising drive up there. But the members got so mad that they donated $7,100 to us. Everywhere I go, the UAW leadership is against us. But you know what bothers me? The UAW Constitution says that wherever there is a union member in need it is your duty and your responsibility to reach out to those people. They're violating their own Constitution.

When Walter Reuther died we had one and a half million members in the UAW. We're down to about half that now. There's something wrong somewhere. They've got all this money up there. The strike fund today in the UAW stands at $900 million. We could have continued to receive our benefits for the next 57 years, and the UAW would not have to put in another dime from any local, and they would still have over $500 million in the strike fund. When they cut our benefits off, there were only three other locals on strike across the United States.

All I want is an answer. I think we deserve that.

President Yokich thinks he can shut me up, he thinks that our membership is going to go away. He obviously doesn't know what a union is. He needs to come down to Kentucky. One of my members wrote to him, he said, "You need to come on down to the picket line."

For 33 months, to this date, there was never a person from the International on our picket line. You know, that makes you stand up and think. I know that there are horror stories from all the different unions, because I've talked to other people from other unions too. Fellow workers, I've been educated in the past 14 months. I found out that what I thought was the greatest movement in the world has something deadly wrong at the top. Not wrong with the unions, but wrong with the people who are leading them.

I think it's time we all get involved, and take our unions back, and make them do what they're supposed to do: represent the workers.

Solidarity Forever, Billy Robinson

On January 15, 2002, Terry Thurman, a representative of the UAW International, called a meeting with the officers of UAW Local 2036. The officers were summoned to Thurman's headquarters in Indianapolis, where Thurman told them emphatically that the UAW would withdraw the benefits from Local 2036. In a meeting that lasted approximately thirty minutes, Thurman informed the 2036 officers that the UAW decided that their strike was unwinnable and that they had lost. He was quoted by one person as saying, "This isn't the first one we've lost, and it won't be the last." When the Local 2036 officers attempted to question the decision or the reasoning, Thurman would just repeat that on January 15 the benefits would cease.

Thurman then went on to say that the International Executive Board had authorized the International vice presidents to act if the local officers did not dump their members into the contract that they continued to vote down. Thurman made it clear that if the members did not ratify the agreement, they would petition the NLRB for a disinterest petition and pull the local charter. If the International pursued that line of action, the members of Local 2036 would no longer be members of the UAW. They would have no choice, since the UAW would strip them of their membership and leave them hanging out to dry.

At this point, UAW members had been on the strike line for forty-six months. According to the UAW Executive Board, the strike at Accuride didn't affect Ford and the other truck manufacturers, so they therefore felt no need to pressure the company into settling with the striking workers. The UAW seemed to think that it was OK to let their members at the surrounding plants handle products turned out by replacement workers while their own members stayed out on a strike line.

One former UAW member who worked at Accuride said the UAW stated that it was "tired of putting money out" in support of the four hundred members manning the picket line. I thought that the money belonged to the members? Let see, four hundred members over even ten years: maybe a half million to a million dollars in dues. Not bad work if you can get it. Of course, after collecting all that money, who wants to go and spend it on the members' behalf? Just like any corporation, when a department is operating in the red continually, it's time to shut that department down. Unions, like companies, have a bottom line, a return on investment they would also like to maintain.

Bill Priest, president of Local 2036, called a meeting of the membership on the Saturday following Thurman's meeting. He needed to inform the membership of the new changes in the rules and what these changes meant for the striking workers of Accuride. He also scheduled another vote of the same contract the membership had voted down several times already. In an effort to get the membership to understand exactly where they stood, Bill Priest explained that the UAW, via Jerry Thurman, was threatening to pull the charter of the local if the membership did not accept a contract they believed was substandard. The members felt that they had just been blindsided by their very own union.

Then, for the final act of treachery by the United Auto Workers, on March 28, 2002, after a four-year lockout of its members, Regional Director Terry Thurman sent a letter to Nate Niemuth, Accuride's attorney and chief labor negotiator. The letter simply stated that the United Auto Workers International and "its Local 2036 hereby disclaim interest in representing hourly employees at the Accuride's Henderson, Kentucky facility."

While members insisted that the company was out to break the union by insisting on language that would render union representation virtually impossible, the final union-buster in this story was the

UAW. Its officials couldn't even follow the language of the constitution they wrote and abandoned their members in need.

With the desertion of the UAW, workers who had been manning the picket lines for the past four years found themselves unemployed; Accuride's plant manager at the time, Audie Hammond, sent a letter to the locked-out workers that the company would maintain the workforce of replacement workers. Now Accuride was "free" to deal with the former employees as "individuals." The company established a list for the locked-out workers to place their names on in hopes of a recall.

The mystery of the Henderson Accuride strike/lockout is why the UAW abandoned its members. What prompted the UAW to send a letter "disclaiming interest"? There were more than four hundred men and women involved in the labor standoff. They had the blessing of the UAW when they had originally authorized the strike four years earlier. The members had voted to go back to work two weeks later when they realized that although the UAW authorized the strike, it had no intention of supporting its own members on the strike line. It was when they attempted to go back, even though they had voted the contract down, that they found themselves locked out. What was the true interest of the UAW during this travesty?

At the time of the Accuride lockout, the UAW was certainly flush enough, so it could not be a case of being unable to send strike pay. And even if it wasn't financially solid, the UAW had workers in place at companies that did business with Accuride; union officials could have placed pressure on Accuride through bigger companies such as Ford and Peterbilt. The UAW had used such tactics before, so it wasn't that they didn't know what to do to assist these members; they just chose not to do it. Instead, they sacrificed four hundred dues-paying members and successfully condemned Local 2036 to extinction.

When asked by their own members why the International failed to provide them with the protection and support that is the bedrock of all union promises, these officials urged the members to "get on with your lives."

One Local 2036 member, Darrel Lemon, summed up many workers' feelings about his union, the UAW, in a letter to the local Henderson paper, *The Gleaner*:

It seems to me that this big dog will eat your food for years but if you need any protection he won't even bark...I feel like an abused orphan. After I gave Accuride 27 of my best years they disowned me, and now, after I supported the UAW for 20 years, they abandoned me. The UAW should be awarded for playing the best April Fool's joke in history!

Local 2036 President Bill Priest was given no warning about the UAW International's action, but on April 2, the UAW officially pulled Local 2036's charter. This brought an end to the strike/lockout and finished twenty years of UAW representation at the plant.

But what did the UAW labor officials gain? No one knows the answer to that question yet.

Chapter 12
UFW Makes Fortune off of Backs of Downtrodden Workers

The United Farmworker's claim to fame was their leader—Cesar Chavez. I was once given a book about his life from a union friend (yes, I have friends both in the union and out). There is also his face plastered on the spoiled that are rallying for the rights of the impoverished as long as it doesn't affect their allowance or party time. That also seems to hold true for the descendants of the famed Cesar Chavez. Apparently, his work is not carried on.

The chant "Si se puede" (Yes, it can be done) was used three decades ago to motivate farmworkers to organize and fight for better working conditions and pay, is still being used by the family of Cesar Chavez only now for their own greed. The Farm workers...forget about it! The Chavez heirs are more interested in fattening their wallets with tax-exempt organizations. Those t-shirts with the face of Cesar on it...totally exploits the work of the passionate man. Most of the money gathered from the sales of the rebellious farm worker go into the pockets of capitalists (his relatives) not the farm workers he fought for. In the end it appears that Cesar Chavez won a battle 40 years ago, but unfortunately not the war. Along with t-shirts, his heirs use the sad story of the farmworkers and their hard life to exploit money from the public and private donations. The money received from all these endeavors have built an empire for the Chavez family. With a bloated payroll that employees many Chavez relatives, the empire does little to bring aid to farm workers who have no decent housing and lack even the most basic health care. And liberals have the audacity to tell me that I lack compassion and unions tell me I am anti-worker? What hypocritical B.S.!

To top it all off, these scam artists also engage in crony capitalism. The money gathered from the many tax exempt organization goes to vendors that are run by family friends. For example, while their members starve and still live in poverty. The Chavez family thru the UFW owns a radio station in Phoenix and prior to the real estate bust, built houses in San Francisco. None of the money trickled down to their own members, which is why unions are so skeptical about the trickledown theory of economics.

Since money has now become the name of the game for the Chavez Empire, they went back to their constitution and changed it. Why limit yourself to collecting from only agricultural workers... that is just chump change, they expanded beyond that. A practice in capitalism at its best....expand and diversify.

Leveraging their Latino roots, the UFW organized new enterprises not related to agriculture. One of the companies they organized was a company based in San Jose that made prefabricated classrooms. The assemblers voted and became members of the UFW. Unfortunately, for the assemblers, soon after the contract was signed the UFW aid and abetted the company in changing the assemblers' job classifications, reclassifying them in a lower wage rate position. That my friend is a union that protects....the employer! Good thing the Chavez Empire gets most of its money from donations instead of membership.

What really took the cake, for an organization that preached unionism and whose founder is plastered across the chest of Occupy Wall Street zombies everywhere, is the 3.2 million dollar National Chavez Center. It was built around the grave of Cesar Chavez in the Tehachapi Mountains and can be rented out for events or you can tour it, a mecca for all budding socialists, communists, and other dead weight. The center was built with non-union labor.

Why stop there, in Bakersfield California, the UFW had purchased an apartment complex and was taking bids. They turned down a bid from a unionized roofing company. Their excuse was that they could get non-union contractors cheaper. I am sure that farm owners say the same thing to those who want to raise the wages of the farm workers. After the roofing company employees launched a protest outside of the apartment complex, the UFW, afraid of bad press reversed itself and hired the unionized roofing company.

Over the past 20 years, the more than 230 million dollars raised by the UFW went to buy or build houses in California, Texas, New Mexico, and Arizona. The homes were not for their members, and with the exception of Bakersfield, not with union labor.

Paul Chavez, one of Cesar's sons, finds using union labor tricky. After all you can house more people if you use cheap labor. How can they offer these excuses with a straight face? According to Chavez their housing projects are aimed at low income families. That is admirable for sure, but the houses that the United Farm Workers union builds by exploiting the conditions of itinerant farmworkers are not for their low income members. No indeed, those people make too little money and intermittent work season make them just a little too objectionable to allow them to be tenants. Is this really legal?

Of course being labeled the United Farm Workers could cause a problem when it comes to marketing their properties so Paul Chavez feels that they should probably change the name of the Farm Workers Service Center into something without the words farm worker in it. He compared it to KFC. When Kentucky Fried Chicken branched out to non-fried foods, they rebranded themselves—KFC—to avoid confusion as to what types of food they offer. Wow sounds very capitalistic to me.

You gotta love this scam. They get their money by selling the plight of the farm worker and then turn it into a profit making machine.

Besides the salaries that Cesar Chavez's relatives pay themselves, the next biggest expense is soliciting for money thru direct mail fundraising letters. Rather than organizing and union elections, the UFW sell memberships. Now you ask, why would anyone buy one if it offers no benefit? Well for the price of $40 you get a laminated I.D., which most farm workers, who are undocumented, lack and need desperately.

Our government could learn a thing or two from the UFW, specifically their spending for social programs. The Martin Luther King Farm Workers Fund was established to provide farm workers with social services such as health care and education. These services were to be provided without cost because of the poverty that these workers lived in. Their mission was one of compassion and in giving a hand up. It was "irrevocably dedicated" in 1975. Such was the importance of this fund, that is was a non-negotiable part of every contract that the UFW negotiated. The standard contribution for an employer was five cents per man-hour. It is a tax-exempt fund that by 2006 had 10 million dollars, which was accumulating interest as it sat in an account. Each year the smallest amount allowed by law is given out to maintain their tax-exempt status in support of the farm worker movement.

The money had not been spent on farmworkers in more than a decade.

Later in 1995, I imagine as a part of rebranding, Paul Chavez changed the name of the fund from the Martin Luther King Farm Workers Fun to the Cesar E. Chavez Community Development Fund. Not so "irrevocably dedicated" after all.

The social services that were once provided through the fund without, now carry a price tag to the farm workers.

As the Chavez Empire grows richer and more influential, (they are firmly in the 1%) in the farmlands and canyons of California, Arizona, New Mexico, and Texas, farm workers live in squalor. They live without indoor plumbing, no drinkable water, and no power.

Arturo Rodriguez, son in law of Cesar Chavez, and president of the UFW acknowledged that, "it's sad down there." Yet the 10 million dollars sat in a bank collecting interest and the United Farm Workers union has done nothing to help the very people work hourly work provided the money.

One good thing to mention about the UFW is unlike the more traditional labor unions, the UFW pension fund is fat and happy with over 100 million dollars in assets. Of course, the reason being that with few contracts, many farm workers never end up being able to qualify for the money put into the fund in their name. In fact, just roughly over 2,300 farm workers are drawing a pension from the fund.

In 2002, Chavez's heirs excised the preamble.

"We, the Farm Workers of America, have tilled the soil, sown the seed and harvested the crops. We have provided food in abundance for the people in the cities, the nation and the world but have not had sufficient food for our own children.... And just as work on the land is arduous, so is the task of building a union. We pledge to struggle as long as it takes to reach our goals."

Chapter 13
Celebrity Sympathizes with Union? Not

Are any union members even a little ticked off at the hypocrisy of celebrities? Just a little? Does it not strike a nerve when you hear Arianna Huffington and Michael Moore bloviate about the oppression of the working people and then become oppressors? How is this OK?

Arianna Huffington rose to fame when her *Huffington Post* was purchased by AOL for a mind-numbing $315 million. Personally I think that AOL got ripped off on that one. However, Arianna has been a vocal crusader for working people, while caustically criticizing corporations and capitalists in her blogs. To start, the Huffington purchase's large ticket price came on the heels of nine hundred AOL staffers losing their jobs. I don't think the Queen of HuffPo lost any sleep for those working people. Then came the strike. Nary a word from Richard Trumka on this slam against union workers.

The CWA, which is known as the Communications Workers of America to the press but in the union world is nicknamed the Marxist Maulers (you can identify them by their red shirts), is calling on Huffington to share the spoils with her bloggers.

Most community blogs offer bloggers a chance to post their articles or blogs, but they seldom pay the bloggers. These blogs give bloggers a place to post information and opinions that otherwise would not get an audience, while the blog in turn is able to offer its readers a variety of postings to keep them coming back. That is generally how it works. However, most community blogs don't get bought for $315 million either, and now those whose blogs made *Huffington Post* worth so much to AOL would like some type of monetary thank you.

Enter the union. Visual Art Source, Artscene, and Art Ltd. form an umbrella art publishing company, VAS, that provides its writers' content to other sites, including the *Huffington Post*. HuffPo pays nothing for these posts. Due to Arianna telling those dedicated bloggers "hell no" when it came to sharing her newly acquired green-backs, they decided to go on strike.

Arianna Huffington, no doubt, doesn't see a need to be coerced into sharing her treasure; after all, the writers knew the deal when they signed on, and with the HuffPo pulling in 26 million viewers, if these bloggers don't want to contribute, it would not be hard to find others who do.

Kinda reminds you of those corporate titans that Ms. Huffington likes to talk smack about, doesn't it?

Obviously the precocious Arianna doesn't feel inclined to share her profits, and yet she still feels comfortable with speaking out for the working class. That woman has cajones.

Huffington even resorted to typical corporate speak when she stated that "there are plenty of people willing to take their place if they do" go out on strike.

"The idea of going on strike when no one really notices," Huffington said. "Go ahead, go on strike."

So, one would ask, why would the CWA enter into a dispute between unpaid bloggers who aren't members of the union and their liberal boss? Well, it seems that unpaid writers are taking work from those who like to get paid. The Newspaper Guild (TNG) represents the paid ones. The unions whose members get paid for writing have seen a drop in work, as well as membership, with all this writing being performed for free. The Newspaper Guild is a subsidiary of CWA. TNG-CWA seemed only too happy to jump in.

TNG-CWA launched a full-fledged strike in support of VAS. The Newspaper Guild called on all its members to "shine a light on the unprofessional and unethical practices" of the *Huffington Post*. They asked all writers not to become scabs or cross any picket lines—in this case, electronic ones.

So let's see how this crazy cycle of the left and unions works. The unions are not only the ground force of the left movement, but the ATM as well. The unions need paid union jobs filled by dues-paying members to be able to continue filling that spot for the left. Without the unions, the left would have to find another massive organized group, and, well, I just don't see anything that can come close to what the union offers now.

Arianna is a tool of the progressive left, and so are the unions; they should be supporting each other. However, with the HuffPo acting like corporate America, the real test is if anyone crosses the picket line to continue to write; if so, they are in effect becoming the thing they abhor most. Huffington is willing to believe that the lefty writers will turn their backs on the unions and cross that electronic picket line.

Everyone on the right, please gather around and welcome Arianna Huffington to the Society of Capitalist Pigs.

Truth is stranger than fiction.

Now, onward to the celeb with the leftist cred: the one, the only Michael Moore, union-buster.

While Michael Moore was in Wisconsin verbally abusing Scott Walker and tea party members alike (with his limited grasp of the English language) for delivering a smack-down on public workers, he never mentioned that he delivered his own union smack-down.

Sad but true, Michael Moore is a union-buster.

He stirred up the masses in Wisconsin with a populist message:

> *America is not broke. Contrary to what those in power would like you to believe so that you'll give up your pension, cut your wages and settle for the life your great-grandparents had. America is not broke. Not by a long shot. The country is awash in wealth and cash. It's just that it is not in your hands.*
>
> *It has been transferred in the greatest heist in American history from the workers and consumers to the banks and portfolios of the uber-rich. Right now this afternoon just 400 Americans have more wealth than half of all Americans combined. Let me say that again, and please someone in the mainstream media, just repeat this fact once. We're not greedy. We'll be happy to hear it just once. 400 obscenely wealthy individuals, 400 little Mubaraks, most of whom benefited in some way from the multi-trillion-dollar taxpayer bailout of 2008,*

now have more cash, stock, and property than the assets of 155 million Americans combined.

Bravo, Mr. Moore, it is evident you are on the wrong side of the camera. Yes, Michael Moore, the hero of the oppressed classes, champion of the 99-percenters, was described by the writers of his NBC television show, *TV Nation,* "as more of a selfish union-busting boss than anything else." His own staff went on to describe Mr. Moore as a man with a carefully constructed facade of a liberal crusader, but underneath the facade lay nothing more than a ruthless, malicious jerk who gave no thought to the "working man."

Yes, the horrifying truth is that Michael Moore is less than the perfect boss. The staff of *Mother Jones* dreaded their exposure to this disgusting charlatan, who was so egocentric he couldn't bear the thought of sharing anything. He didn't share his wealth, his power, or even the credit. In fact, Moore was such an egomaniac that those who didn't agree with him often found themselves terminated.

This control freak would never want his workers represented by a union and, in fact, made it clear he didn't want his writers joining the Writers Guild.

Positively phony. Moore even went on to use the same tactics against his employees that he accused the right of using.

When the Writers Guild kept putting pressure on Moore to reclassify two of his associate producers as writers, Moore told the two writers, who were not members of a union and who did not receive health benefits, "I'm getting a lot of heat from the union to call you guys writers and pay you under the union rules. I don't have the budget for that. But if they keep coming down on me, that'll mean I'll only be able to afford one of you and the other one's gotta go."

No wonder the unions get the shaft, with defenders like these.

Perhaps the unions should start reassessing their alliances. Maybe hold out for at least an engagement ring before giving it up on the first date.

Michael Moore likes to deny that any of the above is true; however, he does seem to have established a pattern of anti-union behavior.

The movie *Capitalism: A Love Story* was filmed with nonunion stagehand workers, as opposed to the Great Deceitful One hiring union workers for the union jobs. The documentary was based on greedy corporate evildoers exploiting innocent, hard-working people. Michael Moore could have pulled from an available pool of union labor for his film, but he chose not to. Perhaps the documentary was based on his personal experience as a boss man.

An unidentified IATSE (International Alliance of Theatrical Stage Employees) member told an ABC reporter, "For all of the different jobs on the movie that could have used union labor, he used union labor, except for one job, the stagehands, represented by IATSE."

Ari Emanuel, Moore's agent and brother of Rahm Emanuel, never denied the IATSE snub in favor of nonunion workers when he released a statement to ABC News.

The use of nonunion labor became such an issue, the American Federation of Teachers refused to accept free movie tickets. The real irony of all this is that while Moore laments the lack of health care for the working class, he failed to provide his nonunion workers with the same benefits.

Michael Moore is a practiced and skillful charlatan who has been able to make money off those he cons with his skillful re-creation as a populist.

I wasn't quite sure where to put this next example of do what I say not as I do, but I decided that it should be here along with Michael Moore. The star of this in your face hypocrisy ids Nancy Pelosi, champion of the little people and all things progressive; the mouth of the liberal elite within the hallowed halls of congress. Pelosi had the gall to state that unions are "fighting for America's working families". In fact, she is so revered by organized labor, that in 2003 Pelosi received the Cesar Chavez Award given by the United Farm Workers. What a shame that Nancy dearest's business enterprises are most notably non-union.

Here defense for being nonunion is hey, I pay more than the unions do. The truth is that the employers that have union represented employees negotiated the lower wage. Pelosi could have had unionized employees and still paid above the other unionized wineries. What Pelosi is not saying is what I will state here. I have often recommended to employers, that to stay union free they should pay as much or more than the unionized competition. Pelosi is providing the economic incentive to her employees not to organize. By her actions, she has shown that it is more beneficial for employees to be non-union. Her spokesperson defended her nonunion winery, which sold grapes to nonunion wine makers by saying it is illegal for Pelosi to approach the union and invite them in. Nevertheless, with a woman who received the Cesar Chavez award you would think the United Farm Workers would have high tailed it up there. I mean I am sure Nancy dearest would not have even called for an election, which is her right. She could have just recognized them once the showed that the majority of the employees supported it.

Along with a non-union winery, we can add these other non-union business ventures. There is a string of Piata restaurants, which I am surprised that they were not organized by the Industrial Workers of the World (Wobblies). After all, they went after Starbucks and Jimmy Johns Gourmet sandwich shop. Pelosi I am sure would sign a neutrality agreement with them so that they could get cards signed from the 900 hundred employees.

Do members want to see what their unions' political donations get them? Pelosi back around 2006 was the Hotel Employees and Restaurant Employees Union favorite politician and they contributed to her campaign more heavily than any other politician. You would recognize them by their acronym, UNITE HERE. So you would think that they would see some instant gratification from the generosity. Oh the humanity, such gratification was not to be. At the time in Napa Valley, a very highbrow exclusive resort, the Napa Valley Auberge Du Soleil Resort is owned by the then Speaker of the House and every one of its 250 employees were non-union. Gee, you think this was an oversight by UNITE HERE?

Book Three
Democrat Stepchild

"The proper business of a labor union is to get higher wages, better hours and good shop conditions for the workmen. But when labor en masse plunks its vote for its own party, then the spirit of party loyalty begins to obscure labor's objectives—high wages, short hours, decent shop conditions. Thus class-conscious labor leaders become more interested in their party welfare than in the fundamental objectives of the labor unions. So we shall have the class-conscious political worker trading his vote not for the immediate objective of wages, hours, and shop conditions, but for power for his political labor boss."
—William Allen White in a speech given September 20, 1937

"I got involved in the labor movement not because I wanted to negotiate wages, but because I saw it as a vehicle to do massive social change to include lots of people."
—Richard Trumka, President, AFL-CIO

Chapter 14
Unions as Environmentalists

When it comes to politics, no special-interest group has sold themselves more cheaply than organized labor. Like a two-bit hooker on a Monday night in a one-horse town, organized labor desperately latches on to any Democrat who glances in their direction.

Union members find themselves fighting among themselves over a social or environmental agenda that they should not even be involved in. While many special-interest groups lobby for their own special interest—hence the name—labor lobbies on behalf of everyone's *except* their members' interest. It does not take a rocket scientist to see that an alliance between environmentalists and trade unions could only end in misery. The marriage was dysfunctional to begin with. What labor leader wants to take credit for that bright idea? Trade unions build things. That's what they do: they construct buildings, roads, public-works projects, and maybe a pipeline or two.

Environmentalists, just for the record, oppose anything being built. They fight against highways, drilling, pipelines, buildings, and anything else that might hurt a tree's feelings. Yet the unions support the environmentalists so much that they should become registered lobbyists for the Greenies. Unfortunately, this whoring-out of their members' grassroots efforts costs union jobs for their members. Of course, that does free up quite a few bodies to participate in marches, so maybe there is a method to their madness.

Quite recently, the unions placed all their eggs in the Barak Obama basket. In return, Obama delivered the Keystone Pipeline to the...wait for it...environmentalists. Yes, like the red-headed step-child of old, organized labor got a big glass of "suck" (coined by a very astute manager when dealing with unions).

"The Administration and environmentalists have blown the whistle on workers trying to feed their families and keep a roof over their heads," said [Laborers' International Union of North America General President Terry] *O'Sullivan. "Instead of celebrating their victory by hugging a tree they should hug a jobless construction worker because they're the ones who are going to need it."*

The controversial 1,700-mile pipeline, which would create thousands of jobs for construction workers, would carry tar sands oil from western Canada to refineries along the Texas Gulf Coast. Its route would take it through eight states, including the environmentally sensitive Nebraska Sandhills Region.

In the battle over the Keystone Pipeline, environmentalists lined up against big labor (which really isn't so big any more if a treehugger can whoop its butt). Actually, that isn't an accurate lineup of sides. The environmentalists and non-trade unions lined up against the building and trade unions. Union solidarity and unity—they don't really mean that; it's just a sound bite, it's not like it's for real, you know. On the side of the building and trade unions were the Republicans—imagine that.

If any union can be proud of its leadership at this point, it is the Laborers' International Union of North America. As LIUNA General President Terry O'Sullivan told *Politico, "The rules have changed. So we'll react accordingly."*

"It's repulsive, it's disgusting and we're not going to stand idly by," LIUNA officials said in pulling out of the BlueGreen Alliance—a coalition of environmental groups and labor unions that represented nearly all the groups that had signed a joint statement backing Obama. (The BlueGreen Alliance itself did not take a position on the pipeline.)

The war of words had now commenced in earnest. *"Unions and environmental groups that have no equity in the work have kicked our members in the teeth,"* O'Sullivan said. *"And anger is an understatement as to how we feel about it. We're not sitting at the same table as people that destroy our members' lives."*

Now let me walk through my thought process with you for a minute. Had the progressive Democrats lined up with the building and trade unions—and as we know, Republicans like pipeline, drilling, and all that—everything would have been copacetic. Instead, the greenies and the unions that reneged on their unity pledges, as well as Democrats who basically said, "We don't need no stinking jobs," now accused Republicans of trying to drive a wedge between labor and their Democratic Party masters.

"It was kind of not explicitly about the president's decision [on the pipeline] but the main issue was to rally around the president when the issue of jobs was being taken over by the GOP," said Sean Sweeney, director of the Global Labor Institute at Cornell University, who helped the effort to stop the pipeline.

Unions representing construction workers who would have directly benefitted from building the pipeline felt stabbed in the back by unions that joined environmental groups to congratulate Obama for killing the project.

"We've worked with Sierra [Club] and the others for a long time and we raised the issues about the hypocrisy of the Republicans in our statement," Communications Workers of America spokeswoman Candice Johnson said. *"That's what we believe and...we thought it was very important to lay out exactly what was happening."*

Remember reading about the CWA earlier? If it was willing to abandon its own members who worked for Verizon, what would make the building and trade unions believe the CWA would support them?

The unions that have come out against the pipeline see it as a project they would not benefit from, so throwing their fellow unions under the bus is the normal protocol. Everyone should have known the steelworkers would poo-poo the idea, since their unionized companies lost the bid to make the pipe for it. Therefore, they were having a toddler tantrum by essentially saying, "If I can't play on the pipeline, no one else can either."

The UAW, the union that brought you the bankruptcy of the American auto industry and the sellout of the Accuride workers, had no problems from the trade unions when it extorted money from taxpayers, but couldn't wait to add its kick-in when the trades needed its help the most.

SEIU, whose officials would be ashamed if they had any conscience at all for bringing America ACORN and a new way of registering nonexistent voters, stood firmly against the pipeline and jobs for their fellow union brothers and sisters, but had no problem insisting on help when they felt the heat in Wisconsin. Which by the way, everyone thought was about the loss of bargaining rights. Not so! SEIU had offered Wisconsin such concessionary terms in a contract leading up to the fight, one could wonder why the employees needed a contract at all. The problem was that Wisconsin insisted on giving their public employees the option of opting out of paying monthly dues. It wasn't workers' rights that sent SEIU to the streets; it was the loss of revenue.

Of course, lest we forget the Amalgamated Transit Union, the Rodney Dangerfield of the union movement, which was successfully decertified by workers at the Wynn Casinos before even managing to get a contract, also sided with the Sierra Club. Remember ATU President Hanley and his henchmen, who thought intimidation was a form of effective labor relations with their own staff? In this case, ATU siding with the Sierra Club actually might help put the trade unions on the other side.

If I were the trade unions, I would be playing "let's make a deal" with Republicans. After all, getting their members back to work should be their first priority; battle with Republicans over labor law later.

It boggles the mind that organized labor, especially the trades, don't see that they are in an abusive relationship. They are constantly getting the smack-down from progressives, and then when the progressives need the bodies for grassroots or money, suddenly it's "I'm sorry, I didn't mean it, it will never happen again." The cycle continues. When will the members of the trade unions realize that the Blue Dog Democrats who actually cared about organized labor went the way of the dodo bird? Progressives view them as a lower class of people: uneducated blue-collar guys who cling to guns, religion, and a Budweiser. The sooner these unions learn the art of negotiations and play hard to get with both political parties, the sooner they can bring home the bacon for their members.

But what I am thinking is that Trumka of the AFL-CIO isn't worried about wages and jobs. At least the AFL-CIO believed that Obama made the wrong call, which is about as harsh as the criticism is going to get. Laborers issued an ominous statement critical of the pipeline decision as *"politics at its worst"* and threatening that *"blue collar construction workers across the U.S. will not forget this."*

I hope they don't. As construction workers sit at home with 16 percent unemployment (1.3 million men and women jobless) hanging over the industry, wondering how they will feed their families and pay their bills, I hope beyond all hope that they stage a rebellion against the far left that knocks them on their asses. Progressives have effectively told the blue-collar worker that a desert rat is more important than they and their families are, and that would make anyone angry.

The unions that came out against jobs for workers did so because in their eyes it was more important to vilify the Republicans and get Obama reelected than to ensure their members had jobs. If jobs and workers' rights aren't the priority of organized labor, what is the point of union representation?

Yeah, I want to belong to a union so it can take my money and use it to support efforts that will cost me my livelihood. Absolutely makes sense to me.

"It's the equivalent of us stepping in when they were doing the bailout of General Motors and saying 'this is bullsh—,'" a pro-pipeline labor official said. *"Nobody wants to step up to help us. Or just stay silent and let us fight our battles."*

The division in the labor movement has reared its ugly head, and unions' own members should wake up and realize that creating jobs has become not as important as supporting progressive, left-leaning ideology.

Terry O'Sullivan said he was:

"repulsed by some of our supposed brothers and sisters lining up with job killers like the Sierra Club and the Natural Resources Defense Council to destroy the lives of working men and women."

"I think discussion is always good," said Larry Cohen, the Communications Workers' president. *"You have to treat disagreements with respect. You have to work hard for unity."*

"On the issues that make or break the labor movement, I don't think the pipeline is one of them," he said. "We think the core of the movement is bargaining and organizing rights."

"If there's legislation or a project that's good for another union, and my members don't have equity in the work, I'm going to be supportive or I'm going to say nothing," O'Sullivan retorted.

When questioned about the division in organized labor over the Keystone Pipeline Project, Trumka told C-SPAN in an interview, *"They are not divided on the pipeline itself, they are divided on how the pipeline is done. I think we are all unanimous by saying we should build the pipeline, but we have to do it consistent with all environmental standards, and I think we can work that out, I really do, and we are for that happening."* Trumka has stated that he supports the Keystone Pipeline Project.

Unions that recognize the pipeline project would be a way to create about twenty thousand jobs for desperate members are: the International Brotherhood of Electrical Workers, the Teamsters, the Building and Construction Trades Department of the AFL-CIO, and the most outspoken union of them all, the Laborers International.

While Trumka questions the credibility of the Republicans' ability to create jobs, the proof that the Democrats refuse to create jobs is evident in the Obama administration's decision on the Keystone Pipeline Project. When will AFL-CIO officials learn that their job is to create union jobs first? They should align with any politician, whether Republican or Democrat, if it is in the best interest of creating union jobs.

James Riddle Hoffa once said, "We have no permanent friends in politics, only permanent principles."

He should know; it was Richard Nixon, a Republican, who pardoned him from prison. Hoffa always paid his debts and in turn supported Nixon in his presidential election. Jimmy Hoffa Sr. was a smart man who knew how to play politics to his advantage. Trumka could learn from the street-smart Hoffa Sr.

When Obama killed the pipeline project, the outspoken Terry O'Sullivan issued this caustic statement:

"The score is Job-Killers, two; American workers, zero. We are completely and totally disappointed. This is politics at its worst. Once again the President has sided with environmentalists instead of blue collar construction workers—even though environmental concerns were more than adequately addressed. Blue collar construction workers across the U.S. will not forget this."

The president's re-election is at stake here," said Sean Sweeney, director of the Global Labor Institute at Cornell University. "There's bigger fish to fry. There's more at stake here than just a pipeline."

Tell that to the unemployed construction worker; he might disagree with you. But then the far-left intelligentsia has nothing but disdain for blue-collar workers, whom they feel are somehow beneath them.

"For America's skilled craft construction professionals, any discussion of the Keystone XL project begins and ends with one word: JOBS," Mark Ayers, past head of the group, wrote in the Huffington Post last November. He noted that "the Keystone pipeline represents the prospect for 20,000 immediate jobs, and as many as 500,000 indirect jobs via a strong economic multiplier effect."

Ayers added that "roughly 14 percent of the American construction workforce is unemployed," a number "significantly higher" than the national average, which has remained above 8 percent for 38 straight months, a post-Depression record.

Chapter 15
Democrats Turn Their Backs on EFCA

The Employee Free Choice Act—a bill introduced in Congress in 2009, but as of this writing not yet passed into law—has been the fantasy of organized labor for many years. On its face, it would be the gift that keeps giving to unions across America. As much as EFCA is organized labor's dream, for businesses in the United States, it is the Armageddon of nightmares.

To put it simply, the EFCA would give a union recognition in a workplace when the union was successful in garnering the majority of employee support through the signing of union representation cards. Employers cried foul, stating that without any way to police this, unions could falsify signatures, intimidate employees into signing cards, and even lie about the purpose of the card that an employee was signing.

However, as much as the hype surrounding the EFCA was centered on the elimination of the secret ballot, the true, darker intentions of the bill were what scared businesses big and small. Tucked into the EFCA was the little clause that forced a government-designed labor contract onto businesses if they failed to reach an agreement with the union within a ninety-day period.

Contrary to popular belief, organized labor has a higher percentage of wins than losses when it comes to union elections. Where they stumble is after the election. There is no law in place that forces a business to agree to any proposal made by a union. The only criteria the current law puts in place is that a business must bargain with the union in good faith. Companies are not forced into anything that they believe will have a negative impact on their business. Consequently, it is in the victorious glow of a post-election battle where unions often lose the war.

The EFCA would have solved this. If the employer and the union could not come to terms within ninety days, the federal government would send in a federal mediator who would take proposals from both sides and then come back with a contract, which the federal mediator had written and would be binding on both sides for twelve months. This would prevent union losses and decertification of membership for failure to achieve a collective bargaining agreement with the employer, which happens frequently.

It is a brilliant bill if you are a supporter of big labor, which has been pushing for its passage since the early 2000s. Barak Obama's campaign promised that the bill would be passed into law, so the unions were more than willing to mobilize their membership into an all-out grassroots effort to get him elected. They must have been giddy when the election results came out in 2008. Not only did they get the presidency, but they had Congress too. Happy days are here again. With the Democrats controlling all of Congress and the presidency occupied by a former SEIU organizing partner, top labor leaders must have been orgasmic that November night. Their time had finally come, and all that hard work getting Democrats elected had paid off.

Which it did—just not for them. Because, let's face it, the progressive elitists really don't give a bloody damn about blue-collar workers. In the two years that the Democrats controlled Washington, they could have pushed the EFCA through, and the Republicans could not have stopped it. But they chose not to, and in 2010 when the tea party launched its own grassroots efforts, unions saw their only chance to see the EFCA become the law of the land slip away. And still, they support the progressive left.

Chapter 16
NAFTA's Blow to Trade Unions

In 1993, President Bill Clinton, a Democrat, signed the North American Free Trade Agreement (NAFTA). NAFTA went into effect on January 1, 1994. A side agreement that did not get much coverage in the mainstream media, the North American Agreement on Labor Cooperation (NAALC), also went into effect. The agreements involved three countries: Canada, Mexico, and the United States. It was an effort to push globalization forward, with the idea that over fifteen years, NAFTA and its little sibling, NAALC, would increase economic growth and decent-paying jobs within all three countries. President Clinton, in an effort to ease the panic that was rolling through organized labor like a tidal wave, negotiated the NAALC. Before that, no written agreements on labor movements within free trade existed.

While the benefits of NAFTA can be argued, there is no question that over the period it has been in place, it has had a negative impact on organized labor. Unlike Canada and the United States, Mexico's track record on employees' rights and protecting workers is not exactly stellar. Labor in Mexico is most definitely cheaper than the cost of labor in Canada or the United States. Several industries saw a sharp decline in labor as whole factories picked up and moved south of the border. Hershey's is a great example of that. The company closed its California-based operations and now makes its chocolate bars in Mexico. Many Teamsters members found themselves unemployed as a result. So, it is no secret that NAFTA has negatively impacted labor union organizing drives in the United States. This is the cost of free trade. Nothing is ever free, and unions paid the price for "free" trade.

The left-wing media, in an effort to carry the Clinton administration's water, pushed off the main pages of newspapers and failed to report on the major networks the news of NAFTA's impact on unions, wages, and workers' rights. One of the stories that was buried was a report commissioned by the Department of Labor. Kate Bronfenbrenner, a researcher at Cornell University who conducted the study, claimed that the Clinton administration sat on it for several months before releasing it.

According to Bronfenbrenner, employers used the threat of *"moving to Mexico' to hold down wages and benefits."* In her report, Bronfenbrenner found that between 1993 and 1995, employers used this illegal maneuver in approximately 50 percent of all union elections that were held, a steep increase from before NAFTA.

Union leaders, repeat after me: "Dems are labor's friends, Dems are labor's friends."

The report went on to say, *"In fact, in several campaigns, the employer used media coverage of the NAFTA debate to threaten the workers that it was fully within the company's power to move the plant to Mexico if workers were to organize."*

By 1997, NAFTA had been in effect for three years, and its report card from the standpoint of organized labor definitely showed a failing grade. In the eyes of unions, many of the fears regarding the exodus of union jobs, difficulty in organizing new facilities, and other workers' rights issues became a reality.

However, when big labor started to wage a war of criticism of NAFTA, they found out what it was like to be on the other side of the lame-stream media when you attack their darling president. The news media immediately swung into action.

A story in the *Los Angeles Times* on June 30, 1997, described NAFTA as *"a sweet deal economically."* The reporter went on to gush that President Clinton *"should have no hesitation in declaring...a success."*

As for those blue-collar workers who paid their monthly dues to a union, which then used that money to get Bill Clinton elected, they could take solace in a July 7, 1997, article in the *U.S. News & World Report* that said, *"a growing number of U.S. companies [have turned] to Mexico for manpower and manufacturing capacity."*

It went on to describe how this was a benefit because it *"may have helped ease the bottlenecks that cause inflation during an economic expansion."*

It allowed for a "relief valve" from inflationary pressure. Readers familiar with media corporate-speak know that "inflation" means higher wages; so *U.S. News* is telling us that NAFTA gives employers "relief" from having to pay workers more.

Even as their concerns are borne out, organizations critical of NAFTA are portrayed as partisan—as in the July 11, 1997, *New York Times* formulation: *"labor unions, environmentalists and other Democratic constituencies"* or *"protectionist."* Trade-policy dissenters are presented as merely wanting to "kill" trade pacts, instead of calling for open discussion of their implications and offering alternative economic visions.

The *Washington Post* was equally upbeat: *"Free trade is good for the U.S. economy,"* it declared on April 27, 1997; it *"helps create jobs that tend to be higher-paying than average,"* and promotes the exports that have *"helped revive the U.S. manufacturing sector."* For workers who "lose out" under the new policy, the *Post*'s remedy is the same glib panacea from 1993: *"retraining"* and *"improved education to create the kind of labor force that will attract long-term investment."*

Not even the boldest booster can deny the bare facts: US exports did increase, by 36 percent to Mexico and 33 percent to Canada, between 1993 and 1996. However, imports increased more—up 83 percent from Mexico and 41 percent from Canada—increasing the US trade deficit by $39 billion.

More than four hundred thousand workers lost jobs later; the media is still selling NAFTA.

The Clinton Administration started doing the back-pedal swing when those import/export numbers came out. In a quiet whisper in early July 1997, the official report claimed that NAFTA had only *"a modest positive effect."* The liberal media, utilizing talking points they received, only gave minimal coverage, and of those stories, none pointed out the apparent negative impact NAFTA was having on blue-collar workers.

In fact, establishment media won't take up the issue of trade pacts' disparate impact on different groups of people—not even when they're handed the opportunity. When more than 150 labor, environmental, and human-rights activists protesting the proposed expansion of NAFTA to Chile rallied in San Francisco on June 26, 1997, they were simply ignored by the city's major dailies, the *Chronicle* and the *Examiner* (*San Francisco Bay Guardian*, 7/2/97).

In 2011 the Teamsters argued against a new version of the South Korea trade agreement that was on the table, calling it the "Son of NAFTA" and claiming it could cost America thousands of jobs.

> *"The United States has lost 5 million jobs since NAFTA, and the last thing America's middle class needs right now is 'Son of NAF-TA,'" said Teamsters General President Jim Hoffa. "We desperately need to reverse direction and protect our economy instead of giving it away to our diplomatic partners. One of the real dangers of this deal is that it gives South Korean multinationals new rights to challenge U.S. laws. Why should a foreign company or investor have more power in this country than our own small businesses?"*

Hoffa, who does not understand the art of negotiating hard like his father, James R. Hoffa, came out with what almost sounds like an apology. While he prostrated himself by first saying how much Teamsters everywhere appreciated President Obama's efforts in renegotiating the trade agreement, he then said, golly gee, we just can't back this one.

Goodness, Jimmy Jr., with a verbal assault like that, Obama must have been quaking at the knees.

The Teamsters believed that this renegotiated agreement (the biggest since NAFTA) would result in approximately 159,000 jobs lost and would create another trade deficit increase for the United States. It would have a critical impact on some of the industries where the United States still held its own, such as electronics and metal products.

> *"This deal would allow so-called 'Korean' cars sold in the United States to be made mostly in other countries because of the ridiculously*

low rule-of-origin requirement," Hoffa said. "I also have serious secu-rity concerns because the deal would cover products assembled in South Korea made with parts from North Korea."

Obama, the man who claims that he will not outsource jobs, did what Mitt Romney would do—he signed the trade agreement with South Korea.

How's that change working for blue-collar workers now?

The numbers from April 2012 were released to the media. Mar-tin Crutsinger of the Associated Press provided the figures:

In one month, the US trade deficit with South Korea tripled. One month! Thank Mr. Obama! Imports from South Korea jumped 15 percent to $5.5 billion in April, while US exports to South Korea fell 12 percent to $3.7 billion. Suddenly, the US trade deficit with Seoul surged to an annual rate of $22 billion.

Surprise! In a rare moment, Jimmy Hoffa Jr. and I are in total agreement.

Why, then, are the Teamsters still backing this man as presi-dent when he has done his best to destroy their base? Unions have become relegated to organizing the fast-food industries. How's that working for you, Hoffa?

Chapter 17
The True Anti-union President

We have heard all about Ronald Reagan and the air-traffic controllers, how because of Reagan, the demise of the unions was written in the stars. Horse hockey!

Let's look at Jimmy Carter.

Jimmy Carter did more to destroy unions during his short one-term presidency than a host of free-trade agreements.

Few people realize that George W. Bush was not the only president with an architect, a.k.a. Karl Rove. In fact, Jimmy Carter had his own architect, Alfred Kahn. Mr. Kahn passed away on December 27, 2010, but he left us with a legacy that has touched a majority of Americans. For those who fly on commercial jets, it touches all of you. Mr. Kahn is "best known as the chief architect and promoter of deregulating the nation's airlines." He was an economist at Cornell University, and President Jimmy Carter employed him.

The upside of Kahn's work is that it enabled thousands of middle-class Americans to travel by air with their families on vacations, and so on, which also led to a boom in the tourist industry by lowering the cost for companies and increasing competition (capitalism at work). Business travelers started to travel more often, also, as the price of a ticket declined and they were offered frequent-flyer benefits. According to the Heritage Foundation, the prices for air travel fell 40 percent over a couple of decades.

It was never Ronald Reagan who was the union-buster, it was Jimmy Carter. Unfortunately, this isn't the "Factor" with Bill O'Reilly, and the spin on this myth has not stopped yet.

Over the last thirty years, the decline of unions can be directly attributed to President Carter and his militia of deregulators. The impact Carter had on unions was devastating, and I don't understand what benefit the unions get from not being honest about it. This is why I believe more and more that unions have become a facade created by the Democrats to fool people into seeing what is not there. They can cry foul over NLRB regulations and the unfair playing field they feel they must play in against big corporate interest, but the truth of the matter is that because of Jimmy Carter, unions will never reach the high point they achieved in the fifties and sixties.

Having been in the union movement, I see many rank-and-file members believing everything their union bosses tell them, unmindful of the fact that the documents just do not bear out that version of history. Ask any union member what is the biggest cause of the decline of the labor movement, and they will respond: the Republican Party and corporate America. Ask them who single-handedly can be held responsible for the collapse of unions. Like parrots, they can only repeat the words they are taught. However, by the time Reagan assumed office, Carter had already struck the final nail into the coffin. Union membership in the private sector was in a free fall.

The strike contingency plan deployed by Reagan in the air-traffic controllers' strike was the one developed by Carter.

Under Carter, the FAA (Federal Aviation Administration) directed a management operation of provocation against union controllers. As maligned as Carter was by the right, and the media's benevolent portrayal of the man, Carter was as ruthless as the next power broker. He was definitely a man with a vision, and his vision was the demise of the Professional Air Traffic Controllers Organization (PATCO). One year before the contract with PATCO was set to expire, President Carter formed the "Management Strike Contingency Force" to be equipped for a union strike. This plan included using "scab," or nonunion, replacement labor.

Reagan just followed his predecessor's strategy.

Anyone you talk to from the union will swear that it was the PATCO strike of the 1980s and a Reagan-appointed National Labor Relations Board that allowed the government to replace the striking air-traffic controllers, which then encouraged the private sector to utilize replacement workers more than they ever had in the past.

Perhaps, but it was Carter's intentions that Reagan carried out. A strange, but convenient, partnership between two presidents from dynamically opposite political sides.

In June 1980, the "misery index" in the United States had reached an all-time high under Jimmy Carter. This milestone would not have been achieved had it not been for Carter's economic and regulatory policies. Carter had put into motion the most devastating regulations to hit the unions since the Taft-Hartley Act of 1947. It was Jimmy Carter whom unions need to thank for the extraordinary weakening of union influence. So, although I hate to rain on the conservative right's victory dance, President Reagan was not the one who struck the unions the fatal blow.

It is true that the NLRB under President Reagan made more employer-favorable decisions than not (which is why they were considered anti-union). But during Regan's whole term. the NLRB did not have the same negative impact that Carter had set in motion during his term as president.

OK, all union members, please say, "Thank you, President Carter."

Along with the deregulation of the airline industry, Carter also signed two other laws that took aim at unions. One was the Motor Carrier Act, which deregulated trucking and crippled Jimmy Hoffa Sr.'s greatest achievement, the National Freight Contract. The second was the Staggers Rail Act, which deregulated the rail industry. Jimmy Carter signed both into law in 1980. These two acts were a severe blow to both the International Brotherhood of Teamsters and the Brotherhood of Locomotive Engineers and Trainmen (BLET).

When President Carter signed the Staggers Rail Act into law, he proclaimed:

> "By stripping away needless and costly regulation in favor of marketplace forces wherever possible, this act will help assure a strong and healthy future for our nation's railroads," the president's signing statement promised. "Consumers can be assured of improved railroads delivering their goods with dispatch."

Unable to stop Carter's deregulatory move, the Teamsters and the American Trucking Association saw their near-monopoly in the trucking industry end.

However, Carter wasn't alone in his move to crush unions. Liberals, including Ralph Nader and Senator Edward Kennedy, vigorously supported deregulation. Yes, you union sycophants, the liberal Democrats are the ones who produced this anti-union atmosphere, and they quite cleverly did it so it would not go into effect until 1981, the first year of the Reagan presidency. Very diabolical...the GOP should be taking notes. However, had Carter won the election he could have carried out the plan without worrying about alienating the unions due to the fact it would have been his second term.

While deregulation resulted in lower costs across the board for both companies and consumers, the Teamsters found its 2.2 million membership slowly decline to 1.4 million after the Motor Carrier Act became law. Much of that membership has been maintained through mergers with unions such as the BLE, which also saw its membership rolls fall off with deregulation.

It may also explain why the Teamsters union and two other unions threw their support behind Ronald Reagan when he ran for office.

In 1982, the AT&T antitrust suit was finally settled, and the ensuing breakup of the monolithic company resulted in the downsizing of hundreds of thousands of union members. These workers were primarily represented by the Communication Workers of America (CWA), which probably explains why they are organizing airlines, and the International Brotherhood of Electrical Workers (IBEW). Fifty-three thousand union members lost their jobs in one year alone. What does this all have to do with Jimmy Carter? The judge who directed the breakup was a Carter appointee, Judge Harold Greene.

If Carter ever felt the need to return to the workforce, he would make a great union-buster.

Despite Reagan getting all of the credit, no president before or since Jimmy Carter engaged in such devastating union busting.

Alfred Kahn, the chief architect of airline deregulation, stated years later: *"I have to concede that the competition that deregulation brought certainly was terribly, terribly hard on the airlines and their unions, who had heretofore enjoyed the benefits of protection from competition under regulation."*

Ted Kennedy should not be forgotten in all this, as his contribution to the weakening of the labor movement would make the most anti-union corporation green with envy. Dear old Teddy packaged himself as the ultra-rich man fighting for the poor blue-collar chump. Friend to unions and poor downtrodden alike.

The tributes made to this man by those blue-collar unions makes me wonder if the union leaders are hypocrites or just plain stupid when it comes to the damage this man inflicted. The "Liberal Lion," as he has been called, pushed for bigger government and more regulation. However, when it came to protecting those unions that had so loyally supported him, Teddy was not so steadfast. Perhaps those unions that lamented his passing should instead take a look at where good old Teddy really stood. The late 1970s really showed the world what Kennedy, friend of blue-collar unions, really thought of the working class.

Carter would not have had any deregulation bills to sign if it hadn't been for Kennedy exerting his incredible influence.

And where would deregulation get its popularity with the consumer if it wasn't for Ralph Nader, the consumer watchdog himself, lending his voice to the effort.

Kennedy also had compatriot in the deregulation trend in a young policy aide by the name of Stephen Breyer. Yes, the same Stephen Breyer who is now a liberal Supreme Court justice. Kennedy held hearing on deregulation, and one of his opening statements was the following; *"Regulators all too often encourage or approve unreasonably high prices, inadequate service, and anti-competitive behavior. The cost of this regulation is always passed on to the consumer. And that cost is astronomical."*

Who would have thought that Kennedy would put smaller government ahead of unions?

The only ally the unions had in the deregulation fad that was sweeping Congress in the seventies was Democratic Senator Howard Cannon of Nevada. At first Cannon held his own hearings and pushed back against Kennedy's desire to deregulate the United States. Kennedy was a charismatic gent, and somehow Cannon was totally swayed and even became the cosponsor of the Airline Deregulation Act of 1978.

In 1980, Kennedy, high on the success of the airlines deregulation, came back to push even harder for the Motor Carrier Act. Teddy was so proud of himself that he even thought to mention these acts as accomplishments in his speech to the National Democratic Convention in 1980. Pundits and historians consider it the best speech he ever delivered. For those not familiar with the speech, the following was pulled from it:

> *"While others talked of free enterprise, it was the Democratic Party that acted and we ended excessive regulation in the airline and trucking industry, and we restored competition to the marketplace. And I take some satisfaction that this deregulation legislation that I sponsored and passed in the Congress of the United States."*

They were so proud of this, why did they then put it all off on President Reagan?

Unions have been the devoted servants of the Democratic Party for decades. Every now and then, a blue-collar union would break ranks, such as the current president of the Teamsters, Jimmy Hoffa Jr., who had a surprise guest in 2001 at the Teamsters' headquarters in Michigan—President George W. Bush.

President Bush started his speech by saying:

> *"Thank you, all. Larry Brennan said there hadn't been a President come to a Teamster rally in 50 years—only he's been long enough to know if that's 50 years. I appreciate it.*
>
> *"And I agree about this: that you've got a good man running the Teamsters in Jimmy Hoffa. I don't know if that will help him or hurt him in his reelection campaign.*
>
> *"Let me tell you another thing about Jimmy Hoffa. He's running a good union. And in an above-board way, in an above-board way. And make no mistake about it, people are beginning to notice, particularly in Washington, DC."*

Bush continued to praise Hoffa and—like a longtime union man—got a gold watch as a gift.

> *"Some folks might have thought they took a risk in inviting a Republican here," Bush said in Detroit. "But I stand before you as a proud American, first and foremost."*

Bush gave Hoffa Jr. a presidential endorsement as president of the Teamsters. Hoffa was seeking a second term in charge of the 1.5 million-member union.

That friendship became short-lived when Bush refused to lift the Department of Justice oversight of the International Brotherhood of Teamsters through the Internal Review Board.

However, the Democratic Party is guilty of being the two-faced friend, as these chapters have revealed. They have repaid their debt to the unions by pulling the rug out from under them every time they come into power. They have done more damage to the union solidarity movement than the Republicans have dreamed of doing. The legislation that the Democrats have pushed through has fattened the wallets of a select few at the expense of the working class, yet union leaders still prostrate themselves at the liberal altar, refusing to see the ultimate sellout in front of their eyes. Meanwhile, European unions look across the "big pond" and wonder why the unions over here have never broken out and endorsed only pure labor party candidates. Hoffa Jr. can say what he wants about the tea party, but it never sold out its members as cheaply as the unions sold out theirs.

The issue for unions will always be those pure trade unionists who believe the central purpose of the labor movement is to represent workers in the workplace and generally oppose the administration's decision and those who see unions as primarily political organizations that have generally supported them. It is also a divide of trade unions, whose members still in large part cling to their guns and religions, and the non-trade unions (SEIU, AFSCME, etc.), who don't even bother to hide that they are more of a social movement than a means of representing workers with their employers.

Trade unions, which needed the Keystone Pipeline, were infuriated that they were abandoned by the Obama administration just when their members most needed the work. The non-trade unions felt that their main priority was to get Obama elected, not create more union jobs.

"So while the decision to not move forward with Keystone XL may 'destroy our members' lives,' as Sullivan put it, political issues, per the Trumka and the liberal left camp, must override concerns about the actual jobs of current union members."

Here's a breakdown of what some of the top unions donated to the Democratic Party in the 2008 and 2010 election cycles:

•The AFL-CIO, whose president, Richard Trumka, orchestrated many of the protests in Madison in January 2012, donated $1.2 million to Democrats in 2008 and $900,000 in 2010.

•The American Federation of State, County, and Municipal employees donated $2.6 million to the Democrats in 2008 and another $2.6 million in 2010.

•The National Education Association donated $2.3 million to Democrats in 2008 and $2.2 million in 2010.

•The Teamsters union donated $2.4 million to Democrats in 2008 and $2.3 million in 2010.

•The SEIU donated $2.6 million to Democrats in 2008 and $1.7 million in 2010.

•The United Brotherhood Carpenters and Joiners donated $2 million to Democrats in 2008 and $2.1 million in 2010.

•The Laborers International Union of North America donated $2.6 million to Democrats in 2008 and $2.2 million in 2010.

•The International Brotherhood of Electrical Workers donated $3.8 million to Democrats in 2008 and $3.2 million in 2010.

•The American Federation of Teachers donated $2.8 million to Democrats in 2008 and $2.7 million in 2010.

•The International Association of Machinists and Aerospace Workers donated $2.5 million to Democrats in 2008 and $2.1 million in 2010.

•The Communication Workers of America, which includes employees from several television and radio stations and other publishing platforms, donated $2.2 million to Democrats in 2008 and $2.1 million in 2010.

•The United Auto Workers donated $2.1 million to Democrats in 2008 and $1.5 million in 2010.

•The United Food and Commercial Workers donated $2.1 million to Democrats in 2008 and $1.9 million in 2010.

When it comes to politics, the UFW does not carry the burden of other labor unions. They have a brand name within the Latino culture and when political consultant Richard Ross took a poll of Latinos in the late 1990's, the UFW came out on top for most trusted name.

BAM! Time to cash in on the name that Cesar built.

In 1998, political consultant Richard Ross showed UFW leaders a statewide poll of Latino voters. The UFW ranked at the top as a name to trust. Richard Ross told his client, the UFW, "This is Gold"

The Chavez family can never be accused of being stupid, the profited of the UFW. While most labor unions were lobbying and contributing their organizations money to politicians and candidates. The UFW was selling itself to the highest bidder.

Starting in 1999, the UFW started running campaigns. They have handled state campaigns since 1999 and business has been good. With the attention on the Hispanic community, the UFW is frequently called on to run political campaigns, and at times the get paid to lobby Hispanic politicians for causes that have nothing to do with workers' rights—like winning approval for an Indian Casino in Caliexico. They were paid $75,000 by the Viejas Tribe, well above minimum wage.

Los Angeles Mayor Antonio Villaraigosa is featured prominently on the UFW website advertising "Sí se puede" wristbands.

All their lobbying and backslapping helped the UFW receive over $10 million in government money.

Book Four
How Unions Became Leftist Organizations

"*It is impossible to bargain collectively with the government.*"
—George Meany, former president of the AFL-CIO, in 1955; his thoughts regarding employees in the public sector being represented by a union

It may surprise many readers when I write that unions were not always leftist movements. Blue Dog Democrats, yes, but this far-left slide, no. At least not for the trades, or skilled crafts, unions. Before they allowed the unskilled, or the SEIU type, unions to subjugate them, most were trade unionists who leaned Democratic, but were NRA card-carrying, God-loving, free thinkers. I wish the trade unions would separate themselves from those whose only concern is overthrowing capitalism.

SEIU marchers in Los Angeles wrapped themselves in the communist flag.

When the labor movement first took root in the United States, it was no secret that the communist labor movement contributed to it. However, there was a huge divide between the types of union. The American Federation of Labor (AFL) was largely made up of skilled craftsmen. They considered themselves trade unionists. Communism and socialism never really took root as an ideology among these unions. A strong belief in American exceptionalism made these skilled workers resistant to the class-struggle argument. The Congress of Industrial Workers (CIO) were not so resistant to communism or socialism; in fact, most of the Communist Party members and socialists populated the CIO. This conglomeration of unions consisted of factory workers—think UAW—and service employees—think SEIU.

The most revered leader of the AFL was George Meany. He presided over the 1955 merger of the AFL with the CIO, which gave us the modern AFL-CIO. He was also very anticommunist.

In the post-World War II 1940s and 1950, a purge of Communist Party members occurred within the AFL and the CIO. Republicans, when passing the Taft Hartley Act in 1946, required all union officers to sign an affidavit that they were not Communists in order for the union to bring a case before the NLRB. George Meany had already banned Communist Party members from membership in the AFL-CIO. That rule stood until John Sweeney took the reins of the AFL-CIO in 1995, and it was one of the first rules he rescinded. Sweeney welcomed Communist Party delegates to positions of power in his federation. As an interesting side note, Barack Obama gave John Sweeney the Medal of Freedom.

"'The radical shift in both leadership and policy is a very positive, even historic change,' wrote CPUSA National Chairman Gus Hall in 1996 after the AFL-CIO convention."

However, that was not the case when George Meany ran the AFL-CIO. After WWII, The fear of communism spreading took hold within the United States and its government. The CIA thought the communists would infiltrate and then influence the labor unions forming in Europe at the end of the war. The CIA recruited the best organization to combat the "Red Scare": the American Federation of Labor (AFL). The CIA was soon directing clandestine operations throughout Europe in attempt to destroy any pro-communist unions.

At the AFL's 1944 convention, the Free Trade Union Committee was formed to assist unions in Europe. George Meany was one of the four major labor leaders who controlled the committee.

The AFL saw its postwar mission in the world as advancing noncommunist trade unionism. Ideally, independent unions were advocates for workers' and human rights. They were also proponents of full-employment policies and vigorously anticommunist.

George Meany hired a former Communist Party leader as right-hand man. Jay Lovestone, however, hated the Communist Party after a falling-out with Joseph Stalin, and it brought the two together.

At one point, Lovestone sent a confidential report on the achievements of the Free Trade Union Committee to Meany in November 1947 that said: "Our trade union programs have penetrated every country in Europe...The AFL has become a world force in the conflict with world Communism in every field affecting international labor."

Along with Jay Lovestone, Irving Brown was the other AFL representative in Europe. Irving and Jay were close friends and made the perfect team for the mission they had been recruited to perform.

Brown said of his duties as the AFL representative: *"I want to build up the non-communist unions in France and Italy and weaken the CGT in France and the CGIL in Italy."*

Seth Lipsky, a *Wall Street Journal* reporter, wrote of Brown: *"He was American labor's leading organizer, philosopher and strategist in the vast contest waged after World War II, in which free working men vied with the communists for control of European labor."*

One year before his death, Irving Brown was awarded the Medal of Freedom, the nation's highest honor for a civilian, by President Ronald Reagan.

So while Reagan awarded a Medal of Freedom to an AFL officer for his anticommunist efforts, Barack Obama award one to the head of the AFL-CIO who embraced communism.

American unions and their members were kept in the dark about the AFL's covert operations in Europe.

Here the split within the union becomes obvious. The pure trade unionists did not see themselves as a social movement. In fact, they are actual proponents of capitalism, as long as they have the ability to negotiate fairly and freely for wages, benefits, and working conditions.

The Teamsters not only supported Richard Nixon, but also threw their weight behind Ronald Reagan, as did the operating engineers union. Richard Nixon pardoned Jimmy Hoffa Sr. and signed OSHA into law.

Jimmy Hoffa Jr. spent more time at the White House during the George W. Bush's first term than he did during Bill Clinton's presidency.

When Clinton passed NAFTA, it was the final straw that broke the camel's back. The leftists began gaining ground within the unions. After all, they could no longer trust the relationship they'd always had with traditional Democratic politicians.

When the unions split from the AFL-CIO in 2005, most onlookers cheered, thinking that it was the start of the end for unions. By depriving the AFL-CIO of some $30 million in dues, the breakaway unions were able to force Sweeney into stepping down. The signs were there, but no one was watching, because no one knows the culture and climate of unions unless he or she has been a real part of one.

No college or university can teach what a very intriguing quasi-nation within our country it is, in fact. Therefore, no one understood what the split between the AFL-CIO and four major unions meant.

It meant a movement was happening.

It was a metamorphosis taking place: the rise of the extreme-left militants within the union.

The election of Trumka from the United Mineworkers to lead the AFL-CIO should have given pause. Trumka, a mine worker-cum-lawyer, admits that being called a socialist is a step up for him. He helped to turn the AFL-CIO away from boosting wages and improving working conditions. Now, the labor federation focuses on recruiting government workers who benefit from higher tax rates and bigger government.

Teamsters are replacing in-house organizers with people from SEIU and the Communist Party, against the wishes of half their members.

Between 2006 and 2009, SEIU contributed more than $4 million to ACORN.

While everyone was cheering labor's demise, Andy Stern was building his "purple ocean" that would produce a "wave" of organizing.

And then, when they finally noticed the SEIU's "purple ocean" and its "wave," they failed to notice a little crazy group of anarchists.

They had been there all the time

Industrial Workers of the World, or Wobblies, as they are called, make SEIU seem downright conservative. Wobblies are a very strange mix of anarchist and communist. They have members who were arrested for being a part of the RNC 8. For those who are unfamiliar with the RNC 8, they were those fun-loving delinquents who were plotting to set off explosives at the Republican National Convention in 2008.

They have a strong belief in confrontation, violence, and sabotage to effect change. This is the last paragraph of their preamble:

It is the historic mission of the working class to do away with capitalism. The army of production must be organized, not only for everyday struggle with capitalists, but also to carry on production when capitalism shall have been overthrown. By organizing industrially, we are forming the structure of the new society within the shell of the old.

Occupy Wall Street: Wobblies and SEIU. Consider these news reports:

- 5 anarchists nabbed in plot to blow up Ohio bridge OWS
- 100 young men vandalized, graffiti, set fires, in Oakland OWS
- Chicago police officer stabbed OWS
- In Portland, police arrested 29-year-old David J. Hodson, an Occupy Portland protester who allegedly threw a Molotov cocktail onto a staircase at Portland's World Trade Center.
- In 2011 a former official of one of the country's most powerful unions, SEIU, has a secret plan to "destabilize" the economy.

Trade unions at their core were more concerned with EFCA than the health care act: one would give them income; the other actually has no impact on them since the majority receive health care through their employers. Many don't like Obamacare. However NAFTA and several other trade agreements weakened the power of trade unions because of loss of members through jobs going overseas, and that opened the door to the far-left influences taking over.

Now backed into the corner, the possibility is strong that the unions will fight a desperate battle to keep those who are on the far left in office.

Appendix 1

The following is the consent decree which allows for oversight of the International Brotherhood of Teamsters by the U.S. Department of Justice

United States District Court

Southern District of New York
United States of America,
Plaintiff,
-V-
ORDER
International Brotherhood of Teamsters,
Chauffeurs, 88 CIV. 4486 (DNE)
Warehousemen and Helpers
of America, AFL-CIO, et al.,

Defendants

WHEREAS, plaintiff United States of America commenced this action on June 28, 1988, by filing a Complaint seeking equitable relief involving the International Brotherhood of Teamsters, AFL-CIO (hereinafter, "the IBT"), pursuant to the civil remedies provisions of the Racketeer Influenced and Corrupt Organizations ("RICO") Act, 18 U.S.C. ß 1964; and

WHEREAS, the Summons and Complaint have been served, answers filed, and pretrial discovery commenced by and between the parties; and

WHEREAS, plaintiff United States of America and defendants IBT and its General Executive Board, William J. McCarthy, Weldon Mathis, Joseph Trerotola, Joseph W. Morgan, Edward M. Lawson, Arnold Weinmeister, Donald Peters, Walter J. Shea, Harold Friedman, Jack D. Cox, Don L. West, Michael J. Riley, Theodore Cozza and Daniel Ligurotis (hereinafter, the "union defendants") have consented to entry of this order; and

WHEREAS, the union defendants acknowledge that there have been allegations, sworn testimony and judicial findings of past problems with La Cosa Nostra corruption of various elements of the IBT; and

WHEREAS, the union defendants agree that it is imperative that the IBT, as the largest trade union in the free world, be maintained democratically, with integrity and for the sole benefit of its members and without unlawful outside influence;

IT IS HEREBY ORDERED AND DECREED That:

COURT JURISDICTION

This Court has jurisdiction over the subject matter of the action, has personal jurisdiction over the parties, and shall retain jurisdiction over this case until further order of the Court.

Upon satisfactory completion and implementation of the terms and conditions of this order, this Court shall entertain a joint motion of the parties hereto for entry of judgment dismissing this action with prejudice and without costs to either party.

DURATION

The authority of the court officers established in paragraph no. 12 herein shall terminate after the certification of the 1991 election results by the Election officer for all IBT International Officers as provided in this Order, except as follows:

The Election Officer and the Administrator shall have the authority to resolve all disputes concerning the conduct and/or results of the election conducted in 1991 under the authority granted to them under paragraph 12(D) herein, the Investigations Officer and the Administrator shall have the authority to investigate and discipline any corruption associated with the conduct and/or results of the elections to be conducted in 1991 under the authority granted them under paragraph 12(A) and (C) herein, so long as said investigation is begun within six months of the final balloting.

The Investigations Officer and the Administrator shall have the authority to resolve to completion and decide all charges filed by the Investigations Officer on or before the date on which the authority granted to them under paragraphs 12(A) and (C) herein terminates pursuant to subparagraph (3) below.

The role and authority provided for in paragraphs 12 and 13 of this Order regarding the Investigations Officer and the Administrator and their relationship with the Independent Review Board shall terminate not later than nine (9) months after the certification of the 1991 election results.

As used herein, the date referred to as "the certification of the 1991 election results" shall be construed to mean either the date upon which the Election Officer certifies the 1991 election results for all IBT International Officers or one month after the final balloting, whichever is shorter.

STATUS OF THE INDIVIDUAL UNION DEFENDANTS

The union defendants herein remain as officers of the IBT, subject to all of the terms herein, including the disciplinary authority of the Court-appointed officers, described in paragraph 12(A) herein.

CHANGES IN THE IBT CONSTITUTION

CHANGES IN THE IBT CONSTITUTION

The portion of Section 6(a) of Article XIX of the IBT Constitution that provides, "Any charge based upon alleged conduct which occurred more than one (1) year prior to the filing of such charge is barred and shall be rejected by the Secretary-Treasurer, except charges based upon the non-payment of dues, assessment and other financial obligations," shall be and herby is amended to provide for a five (5) year period, running from the discovery of the conduct giving rise to the charge. This limitation period shall not apply to any actions taken by the Investigations Officer or the Administrator.

Section 6(a) of Article XIX of the IBT Constitution shall be deemed and is hereby amended to include the following: "Nothing herein shall preclude the General President and/or General Executive Board from suspending a member or officer facing criminal or civil trial while the charges are pending."

Immediately after the conclusion of the IBT elections to be conducted in 1991, Section 8 of Article VI of the IBT Constitution shall be deemed and hereby is amended to provide that a special election be held whenever a vacancy occurs in the office of IBT General President, pursuant to the procedures described later herein for election of IBT General President.

Article IV, Section 2 of the IBT Constitution shall be deemed and is hereby amended to include a new paragraph as follows:

"No candidate for election shall accept or use any contributions or other things of value received from any employers, representative of an employer, foundation, trust or any similar entity. Nothing herein shall be interpreted to prohibit receipt of contributions from fellow employees and members of this International Union. Violation of this provision shall be grounds for removal from office."

(a) The IBT Constitution shall be deemed and hereby is amended to incorporate and conform with all of the terms set forth in this order.

(b) By no later than the conclusion of the IBT convention to be held in 1991, the IBT shall have formally amended the IBT Constitution to incorporate and conform with all of the terms set forth in this order by presenting said terms to the delegates for a vote. If the IBT has not formally so amended the IBT Constitution by that date, the Government retains the right to seek any appropriate action, including enforcement of this order, contempt or reopening this litigation.

PERMANENT INJUNCTION

Defendants William J. McCarthy, Weldon Mathis, Joseph Trerotola, Joseph W. Morgan, Edward M. Lawson, Arnold Weinmeister, Donald Peters, Walter J. Shea, Harold Friedman, Jack D. Cox, Don L. West, Michael J. Riley, Theodore Cozza and Daniel Ligurotis, as well as any other or future IBT General Executive Board members, officers, representatives, members and employees of the IBT, are hereby permanently enjoined from committing any acts of racketeering activity, as defined in 18 U.S.C. ß 1961 et seq., and from knowingly associating with any member or associate of the Colombo Organized Crime Family of La Cosa Nostra, the Genovese Organized Crime Family of La Cosa Nostra, the Gambino Organized Crime Family of La Cosa Nostra, the Lucchese Organized Crime Family of La Cosa Nostra, the Bonnano Organized Crime Family of La Cosa Nostra, any other Organized Crime Families of La Cosa Nostra or any other criminal group, or any person otherwise enjoined from participating in union affairs, and from obstructing or otherwise interfering with the work of the court-appointed officers or the Independent Review Board described herein.

As used herein, the term, "knowingly associating," shall have the same meaning as that term in the context of comparable federal proceedings or federal rules and regulations.

COURT-APPOINTED OFFICERS

The Court shall appoint three (3) officers—an Independent Administrator, an Investigations Officer and an Election Officer—to be
identified and proposed by the Government and the union defendants, to oversee certain operations of the IBT as described herein.
The parties shall jointly propose to the Court at least two persons
for each of these three positions. Such proposal shall be presented
to the Court within four weeks of the date of the entry of this Order, except that for good cause shown such period may be extended
by the Court. Except as otherwise provided herein, the duties of
those three officers shall be the following:

DISCIPLINARY AUTHORITY—From the date of the Administrator's appointment until the termination of the Administrator's
authority as set forth in paragraph 3(3) herein, the Administrator
shall have the same rights and powers as the IBT's General President and/or General Executive Board under the IBT's Constitution
(including Articles VI and XIX thereof) and Title 29 of the United
States Code to discharge those duties which relate to: disciplining
corrupt or dishonest officers, agents, employees or members of the
IBT or any of its affiliated entities (such as IBT Locals, Joint Councils and Area Conferences), and appointing temporary trustees to
run the affairs of any such affiliated entities. The Investigations Officer shall have the authority to investigate the operation of the IBT
or any of its affiliates and, with cause,
To initiate disciplinary charges against any officer, member or employee of the IBT or any of its affiliates in the manner specified for
members under the IBT Constitution and,

To institute trusteeship proceedings for the purpose and in the
manner specified in the IBT Constitution.

Prior to instituting any trusteeship proceeding the Investigations
Officer shall notify the General President of the Investigations
Officer's plan to institute said trusteeship proceeding and the basis

therefore and give the General President ten (10) days to exercise his authority pursuant to the IBT Constitution to institute such trusteeship proceedings. If the General President timely institutes such proceedings and/or a trusteeship is imposed, the Investigations Officer and the Administrator shall have authority to review any action thus taken by the General President and/or any trusteeship imposed thereafter and to modify any aspect of either of the above at any time and in any manner consistent with applicable federal law. If the General President fails to institute trusteeship proceedings within the ten-day period prescribed herein, the Investigations Officer may immediately proceed in accordance with the authority specified above.

When the Investigations Officer files charges, the following procedures shall be observed:

the Investigations Officer shall serve written specific charges upon the person charged;
the person charged shall have at least thirty(30) days prior to hearing to prepare his or her defense;
a fair and impartial hearing shall be conducted before the Administrator;
the person charged may be represented by an IBT member at the hearing; and

the hearing shall be conducted under the rules and procedures generally applicable to labor arbitration hearings.

The Administrator shall preside at hearings in such cases and decide such cases using a "just cause" standard. The Investigations Officer shall present evidence at such hearings. As to decisions of the IBT General Executive Board on disciplinary charges and trusteeship proceedings during the Administrator's tenure, the Administrator shall review all such decisions, with the right to affirm, modify or reverse such decisions and, with respect to trusteeship proceedings, to exercise the authority granted above in this paragraph. Any decision of the Administrator shall be final and binding, subject to the Court's review as provided herein. For a period of up to fourteen (14) days after the Administrator's decision, any person charged or entity placed in trusteeship adversely affected by the decision shall have the right to seek review by this Court of the Administrator's decision. The Administrator shall also have the right to establish and disseminate new guidelines for investigation and discipline of corruption within the IBT. All of the above actions of the Administrator and Investigations Officer shall be in compliance with applicable Federal laws and regulations.

REVIEW AUTHORITY—From the date of the Administrator's appointment until the certification of the IBT elections to be conducted in 1991, the Administrator shall have the authority to veto whenever the Administrator reasonably believes that any of the actions or proposed actions listed below constitutes or furthers an act of racketeering activity within the definition of Title 18 U.S.C. ß 1961, or furthers or contributes to the association directly, or indirectly, of the IBT or any of its members with the LCN or elements thereof:
any expenditures or proposed expenditure of International Union funds or transfer of International Union property approved by any officers, agents, representatives or employees of the IBT,
any contract or proposed contract on behalf of the International Union, other than collective bargaining agreements, and

any appointment or proposed appointments to International Union office of any officer, agent, representative or employee of the IBT.

In any case where the Administrator exercises veto authority, the action or proposed action shall not go forward. The Administrator, upon request of the IBT's General President or General Executive Board, shall, within three (3) days, advise the IBT's General President and/or General Executive Board whichever is applicable, of the reasons for any such veto. For a period of up to fourteen (14) days after the Administrator's decision, the IBT's President and/

or General Executive Board shall have the right to seek review by this Court of the Administrator's decision. The Administrator may prescribe any reasonable mechanism or procedure to provide for the Administrator's review of actions or proposed actions by the IBT, and every officer, agent, representative or employee of the IBT shall comply with such mechanism or procedure.

ACCESS TO INFORMATION—(i) The Investigations Officer shall have the authority to take such reasonable steps that are lawful and necessary in order to be fully informed about the activities of the IBT in accordance with the procedures as herein established. The Investigations Officer shall have the right:

To examine books and records of the IBT and its affiliated, provided the entity to be examined receives three (3) business days advance notice in writing, and said entity has the right to have its representatives present during said examination.

To attend meetings or portions of meetings of the General Executive Board relating in any way to any of the officer's rights or duties as set forth in this Order, provided that prior to any such meeting, the officer shall receive an agenda for the meeting and then give notice to the General President of the officer's anticipated attendance.

To take and require sworn statements or sworn in-person examinations of any officer, member, or employee of the IBT provided the Investigations Officer has reasonable cause to take such a statement and provided further that the person to be examined receives at least ten (10) days advance notice in writing and also has the right to be represented by an IBT member or legal counsel of his or her own choosing, during the course of said examination.

To take, upon notice and application for cause made to this Court, which shall include affidavits in support thereto, and the opportunity for rebuttal affidavits, the sworn statements or sworn in person examination of persons who are agents of the IBT (and not covered in subparagraph (c) above).

To retain an independent auditor to perform audits upon the books and records of the IBT or any of its affiliated entities (not including benefit funds subject to ERISA), provided said entity receives three (3) business days advance notice in writing and said entity has the right to have its representatives present during the conduct of said audit.

The Independent Administrator and the Election Officer shall have the same rights as the Investigations Officer as provided in sections (a), (b), (c) and (d) of C, herein.

The Independent Administrator, Investigations Officer and Election Officer shall each be provided with suitable office space at the IBT headquarters in Washington, D.C.

IBT ELECTION—The IBT Constitution shall be deemed amended, and is hereby amended, to provide for the following new election procedures:
The procedures described herein shall apply to elections of the IBT's General President, General Secretary-Treasurer, International Union Vice Presidents, and International Union Trustees;
Delegates to the IBT International convention at which any International Union officers are nominated or elected shall be chosen by direct rank-and-file secret balloting shortly before the convention (but not more than six months before the convention, except for those delegates elected at local union elections scheduled to be held in the fall of 1990), and with all convention Candidate election voting by secret ballot of each delegate individually;
Delegates shall nominate candidates for eleven (11) Regional Vice Presidents, as follows: Three (3) from the Eastern Conference, three (3) from the Central Conference, two (2) from the Southern Conference, two (2) from the Western Conference, and one (1) from the Canadian Conference. In addition, there shall be nominated candidates for five (5) Vice Presidents to be elected at large. All duly nominated Vice Presidents shall stand for election conducted at local unions on the same ballot and time as the election of General President and General Secretary-Treasurer, as provided herein;

At such an International convention, after the nomination of International Union Vice Presidents and election of Trustees, all delegates shall then vote for nominees for the offices of IBT General President and General Secretary-Treasurer;

To qualify for the ballot for the direct rank-and-file voting for IBT General President, Secretary-Treasurer, and Vice President, candidates must receive at least five (5) percent of the delegate votes at the International convention, for the at large position, or by conference for regional positions, as the case may be;

No person on the ballot for the position of IBT General President may appear on the ballot in the same election year for the position of Secretary-Treasurer; and further no member shall be a candidate for more than one (1) Vice President position;

No less than four (4) months and no more than six (6) months after the International convention at which candidates were nominated, the IBT General President, General Secretary-Treasurer and Vice Presidents shall be elected by direct rank-and-file voting by secret ballot in unionwide, one-member, one-vote elections for each at large position, and conference wide, one-member one-vote elections for each regional position;

All direct rank-and-file voting by secret ballot described above shall be by in-person ballot box voting at local unions or absentee ballot procedures where necessary, in accordance with Department of Labor regulations; and

The current procedures under the IBT Constitution for filling a vacancy between elections in the office of General Secretary-Treasurer, International Trustee, and International Vice President shall remain in effect.

The Election Officer shall supervise the IBT election described above to be conducted in 1991 and any special IBT elections that occur prior to the IBT elections to be conducted in 1991. In advance of each election, the Election Officer shall have the right to distribute materials about the election to the IBT membership. The Election Officer shall supervise the balloting process and certify the election results for each of these elections as promptly as possible after the balloting. Any disputes about the conduct and/or results of elections shall be resolved after hearing by the Administrator.

The union defendants consent to the Election Officer, at Government expense, to supervise the 1996 IBT elections. The union defendants further consent to the U.S. Department of Labor supervising any IBT elections or special elections to be conducted after 1991 for the office of the IBT General President, IBT General Secretary-Treasurer, IBT Vice President, and IBT Trustee.

At the IBT 1991 International Convention, the delegates shall be presented with these aforesaid amendments for vote; provided further that nothing herein shall be deemed or interpreted or applied to abridge the Landrum-Griffin free speech right of any IBT officer, delegate or member, including the parties hereto.

REPORTS TO MEMBERSHIP—The Administrator shall have the authority to distribute materials at reasonable times to the membership of the IBT about the Administrator's activities. The reasonable cost of distribution of these materials shall be borne by the IBT. Moreover, the Administrator shall have the authority to publish a report in each issue of the International Teamster concerning the activities of the Administrator, Investigations Officer and Election Officer.

REPORTS TO THE COURT—The Administrator shall report to the Court whenever the Administrator sees fit but, in any event, shall file with the Court a written report every three (3) months about the activities of the Administrator, Investigations Officer and Election Officer. A copy of all reports to the Court by the Administrator shall be served on plaintiff United States of America, the IBT's General President and duly designated IBT counsel.

HIRING AUTHORITY—The Administrator, the Investigations Officer and the Election Officer shall have the authority to employ accountants, consultants, experts, investigators or any other personnel necessary to assist in the proper discharge of their duties. Moreover, they shall have the authority to designate persons of their choosing to act on their behalf in performing any of their duties, as outlined in subparagraphs above. Whenever any of them wish to designate a person to act on their behalf, they shall give prior written notice of the designation to plaintiff United States of America, and the IBT's General President; and those parties shall then have the right, within fourteen (14) days of receipt of notice, to seek review by this Court of the designation, which shall otherwise take effect fourteen (14) days after receipt of notice.

COMPENSATION AND EXPENSES—The compensation and expenses of the Administrator, the Investigations Officer and the Election Officer (and any designee or persons hired by them) shall be paid by the IBT. Moreover, all costs associated with the activities of these three officials (and any designee or persons hired by them) shall be paid by the IBT. The Administrator, Investigations Officer and Election Officer shall file with the Court (and serve on plaintiff United States of America and the IBT's General President and designated IBT counsel) an application, including an itemized bill, with supporting material, for their services and expenses once every three months. The IBT's General President shall then have fourteen (14) business days following receipt of the above in which to contest the bill before this Court. If the IBT's President fails to contest such a bill within that 14-day period, the IBT shall be obligated to pay the bill. In all disputes concerning the reasonableness of the level or amount of compensation or expense to be paid, the Court and parties shall be guided by the level of payment as authorized and approved by the IBT for the payment of similar services and expenses.

APPLICATION TO THE COURT—The Administrator may make an application to the Court that the Administrator deems warranted. Upon making any application to the Court, the Administrator shall give prior notice to plaintiff United States of America, the IBT's General President and designated IBT counsel and shall serve any submissions filed with the Court on plaintiff United States of America, the IBT's General President and designated IBT counsel. Nothing herein shall be construed as authorizing the parties or the Court-appointed officers to modify, change or amend the terms of this Order.

INDEPENDENT REVIEW BOARD

Following the certification of the 1991 election results, there shall be established and Independent Review Board, (hereinafter, referred to as the "Review Board"). Said Board shall consist of three members, one chosen by the Attorney General of the United States, one chosen by the IBT and a third person chosen by the Attorney General's designee and the IBT's designee. In the event of a vacancy, the replacement shall be selected in the same manner as the person who is being replaced was selected.

The Independent Review Board shall be authorized to hire a sufficient staff of investigators and attorneys to investigate adequately (1) any allegations of corruption, including bribery, embezzlement, extortion, loan sharking, violation of 29 U.S.C. ß530 of the Landrum Griffin Act, Taft-Hartley Criminal violations of Hobbs Act violations, or (2) any allegations of domination or control or influence of any IBT affiliated, member or representative by La Cosa Nostra or any other organized crime entity or group, or (3) any failure to cooperate fully with the Independent Review Board in any investigation of the foregoing.

The Independent Review Board shall exercise such investigative authority as the General President and General Secretary-Treasurer are presently authorized and empowered to exercise pursuant to the IBT Constitution, as well as any and all applicable provisions of law.

All officers, members, employees and representatives of the IBT and its affiliated bodies shall cooperate fully with the Independent

Review Board in the course of any investigation or proceeding undertaken by it. Unreasonable failure to cooperate with the Independent Review Board shall be deemed to be conduct which brings reproach upon the IBT and which is thereby within the Independent Review Board's investigatory and decisional authority.

Upon completion of an investigation, the Independent Review Board shall issue a written report detailing its findings, charges, and recommendations concerning the discipline of union officers, members, employees, and representatives and concerning the placing in trusteeship of any IBT subordinate body. Such written reports shall be available during business hours for public inspection at the IBT office in Washington, D.C.

Any findings, charges, or recommendations of the Independent Review Board regarding discipline or trusteeship matters shall be submitted in writing to an appropriate IBT entity (including designating a matter as an original jurisdiction case for General Executive Board review), with a copy sent to the General President and General Executive Board. The IBT entity to which a matter is referred shall thereupon promptly take whatever action is appropriate under the circumstances, as provided by the IBT Constitution and applicable law. Within 90 days of the referral, that IBT entity must make written findings setting forth the specific action taken and the reasons for that action.

The Independent Review Board shall monitor all matters which it has referred for action if, in its sole judgment, a matter has not been pursued and decided by the IBT entity to which the matter has been referred in a lawful, responsible, or timely matter, or that the resolution proposed by the relevant IBT entity is inadequate under the circumstances, the Independent Review Board shall notify the IBT affiliate involved of its view, and the reasons therefore. A copy of said notice shall be sent by the Independent Review Board, to the General President and the General Executive Board.

Within 10 days of the notice described in paragraph (f) above, the IBT entity involved shall set forth in writing any and all additional actions it has taken and/or will take to correct the defects set forth in said notice and a deadline by which said action may be completed. Immediately thereafter, the Independent Review Board shall issue a written determination concerning the adequacy of the additional action taken and/or proposed by the IBT entity involved. If the Independent Review Board concludes that the IBT entity involved has failed to take or propose satisfactory action to remedy the defects specified by the Independent Review Board's notice, the Independent Review Board shall promptly convene a hearing, after notice to all affected parties. All parties shall be permitted to present any facts, evidence, or testimony which is relevant to the issue before the Independent Review Board. Any such hearing shall be conducted under the rules and procedures generally applicable to labor arbitration hearings.

After a fair hearing has been conducted, the Independent Review Board shall issue a written decision which shall be sent to the General President, each member of the General Executive Board, and all affected parties.

The decision of the Independent Review Board shall be final and binding, and the General Executive Board shall take all action which is necessary to implement said decision, consistent with the IBT Constitution and applicable Federal laws.

The Independent Review Board shall have the right to examine and review the General Executive Board's implementation of the Independent Review Board's decisions; in the event the Independent Review Board is dissatisfied with the General Executive Board's implementation of any of its decisions, the Independent Review Board shall have the authority to take whatever steps are appropriate to insure proper implementation of any such decision.

The Independent Review Board shall be apprised of and have the authority to review any disciplinary or trusteeship decision of the General Executive Board, and shall have the right to affirm, modify, or reverse any such decision. The Independent Review Board's affirmance, modification, or reversal of any such General Executive Board decision shall be in writing and final and binding.

The IBT shall pay all costs and expenses of the Independent Review Board and its staff (including all salaries of Review Board members and staff). Invoices for all such costs and expense shall be directed to the General President for payment.

The Investigations Officer and the Administrator shall continue to exercise the investigatory and disciplinary authority set forth in paragraph 12 above for the limited period set forth in paragraph 3(3) above, provided, however, that the Investigations Officer and the Administrator may, instead, refer any such investigation or disciplinary matter to the Independent Review Board.

The IBT Constitution shall be deemed and hereby is amended to incorporate all of the terms relating to the Independent Review Board set forth above in this paragraph. This amendment shall be presented to the delegates to the 1991 Convention for voted.

INDEMNIFICATION

The IBT shall purchase a policy of insurance in an appropriate amount to protect the Administrator, the Investigations Officer, the Election Officer and persons acting on their behalf from personal liability for any of their actions on behalf of the IBT, the Administrator, the Investigations Officer or the Election Officer. If such insurance is not available, or if the IBT so elects, the IBT shall indemnify the Administrator, Investigations Officer, Election Officer and persons acting on their behalf from any liability (or costs incurred to defend against the imposition of liability) for conduct taken pursuant to this order. That indemnification shall not apply to conduct not taken pursuant to this order. In addition, the Administrator, the Investigations Officer, the Election Officer and any persons designated or hired by them to act on their behalf shall enjoy whatever exemptions from personal liability may exist under the law for court officers.

IBT LEGAL COUNSEL

During the term of office of the court-appointed officers, the IBT General President shall have the right to employ or retain legal counsel to provide consultation and representation to the IBT with respect to this litigation, to negotiate with the appropriate official and to challenge the decisions of the court-appointed officers, and may use union funds to pay for such legal consultation and representation. The Administrator's removal powers and authority over union expenditures shall not apply to such legal consultation and representation.

NON-WAIVER

To the extent that such evidence would be otherwise admissible under the Federal Rules of Evidence, nothing herein shall be construed as a waiver by the United States of America or the United States Department of Labor of its right to offer proof of any allegation contained in the Complaint, Proposed Amended Complaint, declarations or memoranda filed in this action, in any subsequent proceeding which may lawfully be brought.

APPLICATION TO COURT

This Court shall retain jurisdiction to supervise the activities of the Administrator and to entertain any future applications by the Administrator or the parties. This Court shall have exclusive jurisdiction to decide any and all issues relating to the Administrator's actions or authority pursuant to this order. In reviewing actions of the Administrator, the Court shall apply the same standard of review applicable to review of final federal agency action under the Administrative Procedure Act.

FUTURE PRACTICES

The parties intend the provisions set forth herein to govern future IBT practices in those areas. To the extent the IBT wishes to make any changes, constitutional or otherwise, in those provisions, the IBT shall give prior written notice to the plaintiff through the undersigned. If the plaintiff then objects to the proposed changes as inconsistent with the terms and objectives of this order, the change shall not occur; provided, however, that the IBT shall then have the right to seek a determination from this Court, or, after the entry of judgment dismissing this action, from this Court or any other federal court of competent jurisdiction as to whether the proposed change is consistent with the terms and objectives set forth herein.

SCOPE OF ORDER

Except as provided by the terms of this order, nothing else herein shall be construed or interpreted as affecting or modifying: (a) the IBT Constitution; (b) the Bylaws and Constitution of any IBT affiliates; (c) the conduct and operation of the affairs of the IBT or any IBT-affiliated entity or any employee benefit fund as defined in ERISA or trust fund as defined by Section 302(c) of the Labor Management Relations Act, as amended; (d) the receipt of any compensation or benefits lawfully due or vested to any officer, member or employee of the IBT or any of its affiliates and affiliated benefit fund; or (e) the term of office of any elected or appointed IBT officer or any of the officers of any IBT-affiliated entities.

NON-ADMISSION CLAUSE

Nothing herein shall be construed as an admission by any of the individual union defendants of any wrongdoing or breach of any legal or fiduciary duty or obligation in the discharge of their duties as IBT officers and members of the IBT General Executive Board.

FUTURE ACTIONS

Nothing herein shall preclude the United States of America or the United States Department of Labor from taking any appropriate action in regard to any of the union defendants in reliance on federal laws, including an action or motion to require disgorgement of pension, severance or any other retirement benefits of any individual union officer defendant on whom discipline is imposed pursuant to paragraph 12 above.

LIMITS OF ORDER

Nothing herein shall create or confer or is intended to create or confer, any enforceable right, claim or benefit on the part of any person or entity other than to the parties hereto and the court-appointed officers established herein. As to the undersigned defendants hereto, this order supercedes the order of the Court entered on June 28, 1988, as thereafter extended.

EXECUTION

Each of the undersigned individual defendants has read this order and has had an opportunity to consult with counsel before signing the order.

March 14, 1989
DAVID N. EDELSTEIN
United States District Judge

CONSENTED TO:
BENITO ROMANO
United States Attorney
Southern District of New York
One St. Andrew's Plaza

Appendix 2

The following is a letter sent to Occupy Wall Street to voice support from the Industrial Workers of the World (Wobblies). A radical group that promotes the overthrow of capitalism.

General Defense Committee of the Industrial Workers of the World

GDC Central • Post Office Box 180195 • Chicago, Illinois 60618 USA

Email: gdc@iww.org • Telephone: 773.857.1090

2011

Central Administration

Central Secretary-Treasurer

Eric Zenke

Chair of the General Executive Board

Jason Krpan

Steering Committee

Marie Mason

Chuck Bailey

FW Sparrow

To Whom it May Concern;

The General Defense Committee of the Industrial Workers of the World stand in solidarity with our brave brothers and sisters at Occupy Wall Street. We denounce and detest the
intimidation, harassment, and brutality exhibited by the New York Police. The actions of the
police lay bare the true nature of Wall Street and Capitalism.

We call on all those that still retain a sense of humanity to show their support of the working class by refusing to engage in the brutal silencing of dissent. The only individuals who

remain unaffected by the volatility of capitalism, globalization, and the stock market are those who are getting richer from furthering the disparity of all workers through calculated economic calamity. We support all of our brave fellow workers on the front lines of this occupation throughout the United States, and those like it across the world.

We recognize that the true occupying forces are the wealthy ruling classes, their institutions, and the States that legitimize their power. The police and military forces that protect their masters' wealth and power are just as guilty as their masters.

Only by uniting as workers and standing together as a class, can we take back our streets and our workplaces.

To find more information and join the IWW and GDC visit www.iww.org

Donations can also be made to the General Defense Committee at http://store.iww.org/gdcdonations.

Solidarity Forever!

Chuck Bailey

FW Sparrow

Eric Zenke

References

Berlau, John. "Ted Kennedy's Deregulatory Legacy on Airlines and Trucking." Bailout Watch, Culture, Deregulate to Stimulate, Economy, Features, Healthcare, Insurance, Mobility, Nanny State, Personal Liberty, Politics as Usual, Zeitgeist, August 26, 2009.

Berstein, Harry UFW of Today Sows Little Hope, Los Angeles Times,March 30, 1993|César E. Chávez Middle School Biography, http://chavez.cde.ca.gov/ModelCurriculum/Teachers/Lessons/Resources/Biographies/Middle_Level_Biography.aspx

Drews, Katie. "Union Calls Out Another Union for unfair Labor Practices.". 1/2/12 ChicagoUnionNews.com

Hananel, Sam. "SEIU Employees Picket Own Union Over Layoffs." Associated Press, March 28, 2009.

Harris, Malcolm. "Viewpoint: SEIU Staff Fight for Their Union." Labor Notes, Tue, 05/19/2009—10:20am

Jackson, Janine. "Broken Promises, More than 400,000 Lost Jobs Later, Media Still Selling NAFTA." Fair, Fairness and Accuracy in Reporting, (September/October 1997)

Jackson, Shantel. "Ever Free?: NAFTA's Effect on Union Organizing Drives and Minorities and the Potential of FTAA Having a Similar Effect." 4 Scholar: St. Mary's Law Review on Minority Issues, spring 2002.

Jones, Shannon. "Backroom Deals by US Service Unions Strip Workers of Rights, SEIU/UNITE HERE Assume Role of Labor Contractors." May 19, 2008.

Kelber, Harry. AFL-CIO's Dark Past (3), U.S. Labor Secretly Intervened in Europe, Funded to Fight Pro-Communist Unions.

Maher, Kris. "Unions Forge Secret Pacts with Major Employers." May 10, 2008, Wall Street Journal

Munday, Michael F. "UAW Downsizes Its Own Workers." News World Communications, Inc., November 22, 2004.

Thomas, Ralph. Seattle Times Olympia bureau. Paul, Ari. "Locked in an Abusive Relationship, Labor as the Democrats' ATM." Picket, Kerry. "The Watercooler." Washington Times, March 7, 2011.

Made in the USA
Middletown, DE
27 April 2017